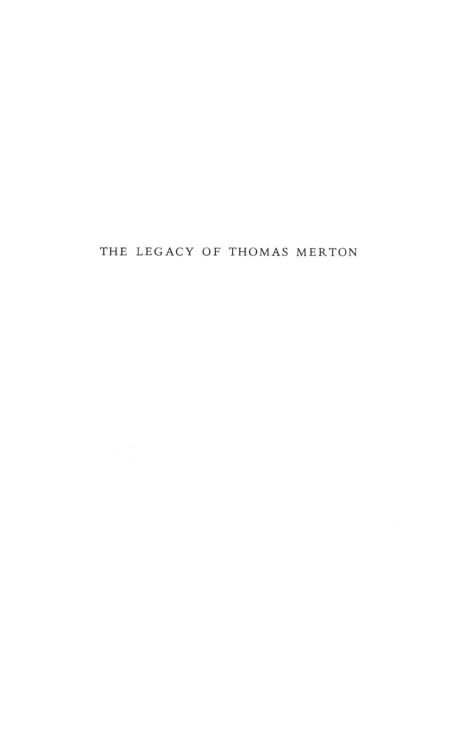

THE LEGACY OF THOMAS MERTON

Woodcut by Lavrans Nielsen
Adapted by Linda Judy

CISTERCIAN FATHERS SERIES: NUMBER NINETY-TWO

The Legacy of Thomas Merton

EDITED BY BROTHER PATRICK HART

Cistercian Publications
Kalamazoo, MI
1986

© Copyright, The Abbey of Gethsemani, 1986

Available in Britain and Europe from
A. R. Mowbray & Co Ltd
St Thomas House   Becket Street
Oxford OX1 1SJ

Available elsewhere from the publisher

Cistercian Publications
WMU Station
Kalamazoo, Michigan 49008

*The work of Cistercian Publications is made possible in part by support
from Western Michigan University.*

*Printed in the United States of America
Typeset by Gale Akins, Kalamazoo*

ISBN (hc) 0 87907 892 8
ISBN (pb) 0 87907 992 4

Library of Congress Cataloging-in-Publication Data
Main entry under title:

The Legacy of Thomas Merton.

(Cistercian Fathers series ; no. 92)
Bibliography: p. 237.
1. Merton, Thomas, 1915-1968—Influence—Addresses,
essays, lectures. I. Hart, Patrick. II. Series.
BX4795.M542L44   1986   271'.125'024   85-30864
ISBN 0-87907-892-8
ISBN 0-87907-992-4 (pbk.)

TO THE MEMORY

OF

THOMAS MERTON

1915 — 1968

ACKNOWLEDGEMENTS

Grateful acknowledgement is made to *Cistercian Studies*, in which ten of these articles were originally published. The introduction was a study included in *Thomas Merton: Prophet in the Belly of a Paradox*, edited by Gerald Twomey. We are indebted to Paulist Press for allowing it to be reprinted here in an edited version. Likewise, we want to thank the editors of *The Canadian Catholic Review* in which Abbot Timothy Kelly's memoir of Thomas Merton first appeared, and to *Monastic Studies* where Brother Patrick Hart's essay on the exchange of letters between Jean Leclercq and Thomas Merton was first published. Finally, a word of thanks to the Trustees of the Merton Legacy Trust for permission to publish short quotations from some unpublished writings of Thomas Merton.

CONTENTS

FOREWORD

As the twentieth anniversary of the death of Thomas Merton approaches, rather than a diminishment of interest in his life and writings, there appears an ever increasing awareness of Merton as a spiritual force in our own time. This is evidenced by the ever wider distribution of his earlier books in paperback editions, and since his death the appearance of a number of collections and posthumous works, including *The Asian Journal of Thomas Merton, The Collected Poems of Thomas Merton* and *The Literary Essays of Thomas Merton.* The monumental authorized biography by Michael Mott entitled *The Seven Mountains of Thomas Merton* undoubtedly is responsible in part for this increased appreciation of his enormous legacy to us.

With the appearance of the Merton letters in a projected four-volume series, under the general editorship of Monsignor William Shannon, an even deeper knowledge of Merton and his message will be accessible to readers of his writings. Eventually (sometime after 1993), the Merton Legacy Trust plans to publish the private journals, until now only made available to the biographer, Michael Mott. These letters and journals will provide an indispensable source and will do much to advance Merton studies.

The present volume, it is hoped, will make a positive contribution in the same direction by bringing together in one volume a dozen significant studies that have appeared during the past decade following the publication of two earlier volumes: *Thomas Merton/Monk: A Monastic Tribute* (revised edition) and *The Message of Thomas Merton.* Published in matching format with the present volume, they comprise a trilogy, and manifest a progression in the field of Merton scholarship.

1

Foreword

The majority of the papers included here first appeared in the quarterly journal, *Cistercian Studies,* during the past ten years. It was felt that these studies warranted a wider audience than was possible in the pages of this rather limited circulation. We are grateful to all the contributors who have so generously cooperated in its production, and trust that its publication will provide greater insight into the life and witness of this twentieth-century monk who continues to be a source of encouragement to all of us on our journeys, whether they be lived inside or outside monastic walls.

P.H.

INTRODUCTION

It is not without significance that Thomas Merton should have entered the Abbey of Gethsemani at a time when Frederic Dunne was Abbot. I have often reflected on this stroke of Divine Providence in bringing Merton's first Abbot from a family of professional printers in Zanesville, Ohio (coincidentally from the same town where Ruth Jenkins, Merton's mother, was born). The fact that Abbot Frederic Dunne had been a book printer and binder by profession made him profoundly sensitive to the importance of the printed word. To the young Thomas Merton, arriving at Gethsemani on December 10, 1941, to begin his novitiate training, the Abbot was predisposed to be appreciative of his gifts. At the time Abbot Frederic confided enthusiastically to one of the brothers: "We have a *real* poet and writer in the novitiate".[1]

The Abbot, as a consequence of his great desire to make the Trappist–Cistercians known in this country, encouraged Fr Louis (the name he was known by in the community) soon after his novitiate to translate biographies of early Cistercian saints from Latin and French. Since Merton knew Latin well, and had majored in modern languages at Cambridge and Columbia, he was well equipped for just this sort of work. Thus, long before Vatican II and its emphasis on monks and religious returning to the sources, to study the works of their founders and early saints, Fr Louis was busy translating obscure lives of Cistercian saints and thus becoming acquainted not only with the Cistercian tradition of the twelfth century, but going back to our monastic ancestors, the pre-Benedictine dwellers of the Egyptian desert, to the early Benedictine monks of Gaul and Italy, as well as the Irish monks and hermits of the fifth and sixth centuries.

My earliest recollections of Thomas Merton when I entered Gethsemani a decade later, in June 1951, were shortly after Merton had been made Master of the Students. He had access to the old vault (where all the valuable manuscripts and rare books were stored) as an office and counseling room for the students. It was a room close to the Guest House refectory in the front wing of the old quadrangle of the monastery. Each time he came walking jauntily down the hall to his vault cell, he pulled out an enormous key, nearly a foot in length, making great gestures as he unlocked the big iron inner doors of the fireproof vault. He usually had a student with him, or one might be waiting outside the door, doubtless for spiritual direction. He gave one the impression of being a happy and spontaneously friendly monk.

As Master of Students at Gethsemani, Fr Louis very soon began to emphasize the need for more opportunities for solitude and to help the young monks in their desire for contemplative prayer. With about two hundred monks in the community at the time, it was difficult enough to find a quiet place to be alone, since we were only permitted outside the relatively small enclosure if work in the fields or the vast woods brought us there.

During the course of an official visitation from the Abbot General of the Order, Fr Louis made a strong plea to have the enclosure extended to include a small wooded knoll on the east side of the enclosure wall. To everyone's great surprise, he was successful in this attempt, and thus on Sundays and feast days the students were allowed to go out to the woods for several hours of prayer or *lectio divina* or simple relaxation in this beautiful natural setting. Not long afterward the novices were likewise given a similar permission, and a wooded area and lake south of the enclosure wall was reserved for them.

This was meant to give the young monks more opportunities for solitude and thus restore the contemplative dimension to the monastic life which had been obscured formerly by an overemphasis on penance and work and an overly ornate liturgy.

Aside from his gifts and abilities as a translator, his knowledge of French, German, Spanish and Italian put him in contact with many of the new currents of thought in monastic and theological circles long before others in the community were aware of their existence. He kept abreast of all the finest journals emanating from Europe at this time. As it developed, Merton began to initiate his own monastic renewal at Gethsemani in the early 1950s by giving conferences on the Cistercian Fathers. This work brought him into direct contact with the four great "Cistercian evangelists": St Bernard of Clairvaux, William of St Thierry, Guerric of Igny and Aelred of Rievaulx, as well as many lesser-known monastic writers. He went far beyond Rancé and the Reform of La Trappe to the earliest Cistercian Fathers of the twelfth century. Naturally, this was received as a breath of fresh air for the community at Gethsemani, and soon spread to other monastic communities in this country and abroad.

In 1955 Thomas Merton was appointed Master of Novices, after having been Master of the Students for just four years. He was to hold this responsible position for another ten years. During this period he had a tremendous influence on the lives of the young men who entered the monastery, and along with the Abbot he was actually responsible for their monastic training and formation. This enabled him to view, sometimes critically, certain methods used in the past, and thus he launched a novitiate training program of his own.

Merton delved into the monastic sources, studying the Cistercian Fathers with the novices and discussing them in open dialogue. Thanks to his insistence, more time was given to *lectio divina,* although manual labor was not neglected. Merton felt, however, that in the past too much emphasis had been placed on manual labor, to the detriment of a fruitful *lectio divina,* meditative reading, study and personal prayer.

Notes of the talks and conferences by Father Louis were

subsequently typed up, mimeographed and circulated to many other communities, once the monastic grapevine spread the word of Merton's pioneering efforts at Gethsemani. Thus, before long, copies of the notes on "monastic orientation" which covered the years from 1951 to 1955 were bound in six volumes and circulated to Benedictine and Cistercian houses in this country and abroad. Beginning with his first year as Novice Master, there were the "Lectures on Cassian" which were soon followed by his own commentary on the *Rule* of St Benedict. About this time his introductory course on the Scriptures in the monastic tradition (especially St Paul) was given and two volumes of notes on the "Liturgical Seasons" appeared. In 1961 he launched a series of conferences on "Ascetical and Mystical Theology" and in 1963 began a course on "The Cistercian Fathers and Their Monastic Theology". Conferences during 1963 and 1964 were on "Pre-Benedictine Monasticism", including the Celtic monastic tradition that he found so fascinating. This gives some idea of the broad terrain covered by Merton in these monastic conferences.

Thomas Merton at the very outset of any discussion on monastic renewal was careful to make the proper distinctions in regard to a renewal that was appropriate for monastic communities in contrast to that which was more proper for active religious congregations and societies. In a memorandum on monastic renewal, which was published posthumously, he made this point quite clear: "In monastic reform, care should be taken first of all to maintain or restore the special character of the monastic vocation. The monastic life must not be evaluated in terms of active religious life, and the monastic orders should not be equated with other religious institutes, clerical or otherwise".[2] He went on to stress the point that the monastic community does not ideally exist for the sake of any apostolic or educational work, even as a secondary end. "The works of the monk are not justified by their external results but only by their relevance to his monastic life alone with God. They are meaningful insofar as they

6

are appropriate to a life out of this world, which is also a life of compassion for those who remain in the world, and of prayer for the salvation of the world".[3]

When discussing monastic renewal, Merton always pointed out the fact that the doors (and windows) of the cenobitic monastic community must be opened out into the desert. He believed strongly that there must be room for those monks who felt a growing need for a greater measure of silence and solitude in their lives as they matured in the monastic life. "Monastic superiors should be ready to see and encourage in their subjects any exceptional and genuine desire for a deeper life of prayer and for a return to a simpler monastic way".[4] Merton pointed out that it was the Abbot's responsibility to foster the spiritual growth of each member of his community. "The Abbot is responsible to God for the development and true sanctification of his monks. When therefore they believe they should seek a simpler, more solitary and more fervent life of prayer, they should not be prevented from investigating reasonable possibilities of doing so . . . but should be helped in various ways to test their abilities and prove the reality of their higher vocation".[5]

Thus Merton saw the possibility of a more solitary life within the context of the traditional monastic community as an important point in renewal. It was a matter of giving precedence to the personal charism of an individual monk over that of the institution. In other words, a true eremitical vocation that might develop and grow within the cenobitic community should be encouraged if it were considered authentic by a monk's spiritual director and his superior. Merton wrote a number of articles on the history of eremitism within the *ordo monasticus,* showing clearly that from its very beginning some monks of the Cistercian Order, after many years in the community, in later life became hermits and solitaries. This was even in evidence at La Trappe during the time of Rancé. These published pleas for a renewal of the ancient tradition paved the way for an eventual approval by

hermit within the community

the General Chapter of the Order allowing monks this option after being well-tried in the community, and with the Abbot's approval, as St Benedict in his *Rule* provides.

Merton's Abbot, James Fox, during the General Chapter of 1965 successfully presented the issue of the possibility of hermits within the Order. His efforts bore fruit, and within a few years Dom James himself resigned his office as Abbot of Gethsemani and became a hermit on the property of Gethsemani. Consequently, the hermit vocation is accepted in monastic communities, although it will always remain a rare calling and few will leave the ranks of the community for the solitary combat of the desert.

One may legitimately ask the question: how was Merton able to keep in touch with all the various monastic experiments and efforts at renewal in other areas of the world, isolated as he was in his monastery in the hills of Kentucky? In actual fact, if one examines his voluminous correspondence over the years, one sees a large segment directed to monks and nuns of Europe and America, Benedictines, Camaldolese, Carthusians and of course Cistercians. For example, his correspondence with the eminent Benedictine scholar and historian, Father Jean Leclercq of Luxembourg, dates back to 1950 and continued unabated until the time of Merton's death in Bangkok, Thailand, in 1968. The early letters are full of questions about new experiments in the foundations in Africa and Asia.

In this country the experiment of Dom Damasus Winzen at Mount Saviour near Elmira, New York, impressed Merton deeply. Mount Saviour symbolized for him what was best in the early monastic experiments in this country in the early 1950s. Dom Damasus believed in a simple type of Benedictine monastery, without parishes or a school and/or seminary attached. Dom Damasus, however, held firmly to traditional monastic hospitality and consequently provided for a large guest house. But he believed it essential that monks earn their living by their own hands by farming, with their life centered around a simple but beautiful vernacular liturgy. And above all, he envisioned only one class of monks. (This idea eventually found favor with other Benedictines and the Cistercian Order as a whole, when their General Chapters abolished the two classes of monks, thus unifying their respective communities.)

It was the policy at Mount Saviour to ordain only enough priests to take care of the liturgical needs of the community, unlike the prevalent custom in Trappist–Cistercian monasteries at that time. A number of Merton's letters to a monk of St John's Abbey, Collegeville, touch on the subject of monks remaining simple monks, rather than clerics destined for the priesthood almost automatically. Writing to Father Ronald Roloff concerning monks not seeking ordination to the priesthood, in a letter dated November 13, 1962, he observed: "Already for some time we have been insisting that the important thing in the choice of vocations for our choir monks was the monastic vocation, not the call to the priesthood. Also, many of the novices have freely admitted that they really prefer to be simple monks and not priests".[6] He pointed out to his correspondent that until a few months previous we had not tolerated this, but since the recent General Chapter it was agreed to try it as a part of the new monastic program. He went on to say: "Hence, we now have a half-dozen newly professed who are going ahead with the explicit intention of remaining simple monks and not becoming priests. They are the best in the house actually. I do not know if they will all manage to have their desire; some may have to be ordained later, just because they do have qualities that make for superiorship, etc. But for my part I would personally support such a one all the way and would encourage him to remain a simple monk insofar as it was possible".[7]

Another subject treated in this same letter was that of a new approach to monastic formation at Gethsemani. It spanned a longer period than in the past, and was geared more specifically for monks, rather than seminarians or priests in the secular ministry. In other words, these studies would concentrate on subjects germane to the monastic vocation: Scripture, patrology and a kind of monastic theology tailored specifically for monks. Instead of three years of simple vows, the Order began to allow for as much as six years. He explained: "After the novitiate, all the choir monks, whether they will eventually go on to the priesthood or not, *continue their purely monastic formation.* This is what we all here consider to be the really important point. They will not begin clerical studies for at least three years after the novitiate".[8] Merton then outlined a pet plan of his own to develop a monastic pre-philosophy course which would have nothing to do with the manuals, "but will be a sort of *lectio divina* of texts from St Anselm, St Augustine, Boethius, and so on. This would be a very interesting course and very important. This would not be until the third year. Before that they will take nothing but Scripture, monastic history, the Fathers and a language".[9]

Personal relationships within the monastic community were another very important consideration in Merton's view of renewal. Writing on the subject of "Openness and Cloister" he concluded that in the past the structures of the contemplative life had acquired too much rigidity and uniformity. He felt there was too much emphasis placed on exterior regularity and on uniform observance which tended to stifle personal development and did not take sufficient account of a monk's personal needs. "Contemplative openness must develop not only in relation to the outside world, but also, and above all, within the community itself. Free and spontaneous contacts between the religious themselves are absolutely necessary. Religious must communicate frankly and sincerely in a personal way and not only in the set of formalized relationships which have been favored in the past".[10] Merton went on to stress the importance of relationships being more "natural" and human, which inevitably would result in a greater freedom and openness in communicating with one another.

But as in so many other cases, Merton balanced this very well with an insistence on a measure of solitude and silence for those whose spiritual growth demanded more of this: "On the other hand, to balance this freedom of communication, the legitimate needs of individual religious for greater solitude and silence must also be respected". He felt that a monastic community (or any community for that matter) which is growing in charity and self-understanding will spontaneously recognize the special needs of its members, and in a spirit of charity strive to accommodate them. Merton added that the mature contemplative (who may not always necessarily be the most brilliant or gifted person in the community) "can contribute a great deal to the common life by his or her silent and solitary prayer. Even those who are not yet fully formed need the experience of periods of solitude and silence in order to grow in the life of prayer. Contemplative communities should recognize the value of encouraging these personal aspirations".[11]

Turning for a moment to Merton's poetry, his early Gethsemani poems celebrate monastic life in all its aspects: "Trappists, Working", "Trappist Abbey: Matins", and "Evening: Zero Weather". One realizes the profound effect that the liturgical life had on this young monk, and how it was intended to transform the entire life of the monk. These poems reflect the early Merton perfectly at peace in his natural setting in the hills of Kentucky. In "A Practical Program for Monks", one of his later poems (written about 1958, consequently after he had been four years Master of Juniors and two years as Master of Novices), the poet complains about the attention accorded to externals, not without a bit of humor. The poem is a protest against an overemphasis on rules and regulations which tend to distort the simple contemplative life of solitude and prayer. Merton's frustration shows through in this poem as he ironically contrasts the highly structured, regimented life with the ideal contemplative life:

> Plenty of bread for everyone between prayers and the
> psalter: will you recite another?
> *Merci,* and *Miserere.*
> Always mind both the clock and the Abbot until
> eternity.
> *Miserere.*
>
> Details of the Rule are all liquid and solid. What canon
> was the first to announce regimentation before us.?
> Mind the step on the way down![12]

Another area of monastic renewal about which Merton wrote and spoke was traditional monastic hospitality. Before ecumenical dialogue became fashionable, Merton began to see small groups of non-Catholic seminarians and college students, as well as artists, poets, intellectuals, and pacifists, including non-Christians. Among the latter were Zen Buddhist monks, Sufis, Jewish rabbis and a host of others. Merton felt that it was important for monks to have some contact with these people, who in turn would influence others of their own group and beyond. Actually, he began meeting with groups of Baptist and Episcopalian and Disciples of Christ seminarians in the late 1950s and early 1960s. He made himself available to them, usually giving them an address of welcome, telling them something of the monastic life, and then opening the forum to discussion, which was always quite lively. He became very popular in this area, and as a consequence after several years had to call for help from some of the other monks. Having come from a non-Catholic background himself, and with his tremendous interest in Eastern monasticism, he was able to empathize with these groups in a way many other monks could not, which helps to explain his singular success.

Merton summarized succinctly his thought in this matter in "Letter to a Priest", which was published in *Seeds of Destruction,* concerning the Rahnerian diaspora situation:

"What am I trying to say about the monk is perhaps too paradoxical and too outrageous to be clear, let alone acceptable: but I think the monastic state should be one of complete liberty from the pressures and confusions of 'the world' in the bad sense of the word, and even from the more 'worldly' side of the Church, so that the monk, isolated and at liberty, can on the one hand give himself to God and to the Word of God, attain to a truly Christian understanding of the needs and sufferings of the men of his time (from his special vantage point of poverty, labor, solitude and insecurity) and also enter into dialogue with those who are not monks and not even Christians".[13]

He constantly stressed the need for monks in their efforts at renewal to examine and return to the sources of their tradition. Writing on the subject of ecumenism and monastic renewal, Merton was later to explain: "The problem of monastic renewal, at the deepest level, is theological, and it is at this point that the monks are finally coming face to face with Luther's challenge. In 'returning to the sources' they are only doing in a more thorough and systematic way what Luther himself did by reexamining his vocation in the light of the Gospel and the Pauline Epistles".[14] Merton then pointed out that monks and nuns today, studying the original monastic sources, seen in their historical and cultural contexts, must begin to ask themselves much more disturbing questions than simply those which are endemic to their monastic observance: "It is no longer just a matter of recovering a genuine understanding of monastic enclosure, silence, worship, fasting and trying to adapt these to a modern situation. The very concept of a vowed and cloistered life, of a life devoted to prayer apart from the world, of silence and asceticism, has to be reexamined".[15]

Merton then sounded a warning to facile proponents of renewal, fearing that those not well grounded in a solid monastic tradition would end up discarding things of perennial value, thus impoverishing and trivializing monasticism:

"Let us admit that quite possibly if we are too ready to sacrifice silence, solitude, etc., we may quickly find ourselves deserted by vocations".[16] On the other hand, he believed a certain amount of adaptation was necessary to meet the needs of the time, thus making the monastic life viable for many who would not otherwise be attracted to this way. "But also if by relinquishing my own favorite interpretation of what the perfect life of silence and contemplation ought to be and submitting to certain adaptations I can make the monastic life possible for others who would not otherwise be able to live it, then it would seem that charity itself ought to tell me that this 'need' of others is an appeal to my own generosity, in a way very different from that which I anticipated when I made my vows".[17]

Speaking about the monastic dialogue with the world and the relevance of monastic life for the future, Merton insisted that everything depended on the *quality* of the lives of the monks today, and the seriousness with which they examined their witness in terms of the ensuing generations of monks: "Monastic life will remain relevant to the future, specifically in the next two generations, insofar as monasteries open themselves to dialogue and exchange with the intellectual community. But for this dialogue to be meaningful, the intellectual community must find in the monasteries both a monastic reality (people of depth and simplicity who have acquired the values of monasticism by living them) and openness to social reality of the twentieth century".[18]

Again, Merton emphasized the need for inner transformation, for without a real and deep spiritual renewal, the exterior changes would avail but little. He saw this combining of real monastic depth and openness to the living intellectual and cultural forces of our times as requiring a special charism. In the thought of Merton, a charism was a gift one must struggle with to deserve as well as preserve. He felt the most basic and important monastic charism is the essential calling to prayer and renunciation and inner transformation. Toward the end of his life, Merton became more and more concerned with the subject of transformation of consciousness, which was in current usage at that time.

If monks were not genuinely authentic and deep men of prayer and at the same time men of compassion and concern for the anguish of the world, Merton felt their witness would be of little value and perhaps cause more harm than good to those coming to seek their counsel and help. He suggested in this context: "If our monasteries are truly centers of deeply experienced monastic life, those who are most alive in the outside world will spontaneously come to share our silence and discuss with us their own fruitful insights. It is this exchange and participation which I believe to be of decisive importance for monasteries. But it all depends on solitude and prayer".[19]

Writing on the necessity of the individual monk to begin where he found himself, and not depend on or wait for communal renewal, Merton stated realistically that what one needs to do is start a conversion and a new life oneself, insofar as one can. "My work for renewal takes place strictly in my own situation here, not as a struggle with the institution from which I am relatively free now as a hermit, but in an effort to renew my life of prayer in a whole new context, with a whole new understanding of what the contemplative life means and demands. Creativity has to begin with me and I cannot sit here wasting time urging the monastic institution to become creative and prophetic . . . ".[20]

This realistic approach was typical of Merton in his later years, after many of his earlier idealistic illusions evaporated. In the last analysis it all depended on how each monk personally responded to his call, his special graces of vocation. The point was well made in the following passage: "What each one of us has to do, and what I have to do, is to buckle down and really start investigating new possibilities in our own life; and if new possibilities mean radical changes, all right. Maybe we need radical changes for which we have to struggle and sweat some blood. Above all we must be more attentive to God's way and God's time, and give everything when it is really demanded. But, on the other hand, let these be real changes and not just neurotic upheavel".[21]

The essential monastic experience, as Merton saw it, was centered on love. He knew from monastic tradition, and especially from the Cistercian twelfth-century writers like St Bernard of Clairvaux and William of St Thierry, that ideally the monastic life was considered a "school of love" or "charity's own school". He resonates the teachings of the Cistercian Fathers in the following passage: "Love alone is enough, regardless of whether it produces anything. In the so-called contemplative life, love is sufficient to itself. It does of course work, it does of course do things; but in our life the emphasis is on love above everything else, on faith above everything else. Especially faith above works".[22]

As Merton grew older and wiser in the monastic life, he depended more and more on the mercy of God, as he often confessed. That is why he loved so much the English mystic, Julian of Norwich, whom he preferred in his later years to the Spanish mystics, St John of the Cross and St Teresa of Avila, with whom he was so taken in his early monastic life. "The characteristic of our life is that it makes us realize how much we depend directly on God by faith. How much we depend directly upon the mercy of God, how much we depend upon receiving everything directly through Him, and not through the mediation of our own activity. So that while we continue to act, we act in such a way that this consciousness of dependence on God is greater, more continual, more all-embracing and more satisfactory than it is in the active life. This is what we really seek".[23]

After the appearance of a provocative article in the *National Catholic Reporter* in December 1967 by Colman McCarthy, Merton wrote a letter to the editor early in 1968 in which he said: "The monastic charism is a charism of freedom: including the freedom not to count in the world and not to get visible results in it. The freedom not to have to talk if you don't want to. Not to have to pronounce judgment on anything. Or contrariwise, to speak out without hesitation when you think something has to be said".[24]

Merton then spelled out the implications of the monk's charism of freedom: "Above all the monastic charism is a freedom from set routine official tasks, a freedom from the treadmill of putting out a superfluous religious magazine, of preaching retreats that are driving nuns stark mad, of bullying married couples . . . . ".[25] Rather, Merton got to the heart of the monastic vocation by saying that a monk does not have to do any of these things, not simply because he has a secret nobody else possesses, but rather "because he is liberated from the need to produce anything by which to justify himself in the eyes of other men. He is not accountable to them for his life because it is something that cannot be drawn up on a balance sheet for anybody's inspection. The 'solitude' of the monk is the loneliness of being accountable directly to God for something he does not quite understand himself".[26]

At the root of this emphasis on the solitude of the monk, the person of contemplative prayer, was Merton's firm conviction that it was more important for the monk *to be* than to do or to act, especially when he was speaking of the monastic ideal in a time of renewal and change. He wanted to be sure that critics of renewal kept this in mind. He disagreed with many critics of monasticism who would have monks abandon their monastic solitude and become more involved in the active ministry, and thus open the doors of the monastery to the world, taking a much more cautious view. He did, indeed, see a need for more openness than in the past, so that guests could come to the monastery for retreats or perhaps to obtain help in their prayer life by those qualified among the monks to advise. But he was opposed to the idea of turning the monastery into a counseling center or a mini-parish church. The monastery had its own particular function in the mystical body of Christ, the Church, and as long as it was faithful to this charism, the more profitable it would be for the Church and the world.

Thomas Merton certainly believed that renewal must come from the ranks of monks and nuns, the grassroots, rather than from the higher echelons. Writing on the Council and monasticism shortly after the close of Vatican II, Merton stated: "While the major superiors and the competent Councils and Chapters must of course finally decide what adaptations are to be put into effect, in accordance with the Rule and Constitutions, it is nevertheless essential that all the members should actively participate in such tasks as: estimation of the meaning and value of their vocation, clarification of the relevance of their particular religious ideal for themselves and their time, evaluation of the contribution they might make to the understanding and aid of the contemporary world, defining the relevance in a present-day context of certain observances belonging to the past, and bringing to the attention of Superiors the real everyday needs and problems of subjects".[27]

The theological implications were clear to Merton who saw this approach as not only pragmatic, but in accord with the new perspectives on the Church. Indeed, we must recognize that "all true renewal must be the work of the Holy Spirit and that the Holy Spirit cannot be said to work exclusively 'from the top down', manifesting the will of God only to higher superiors and, further down, granting to subjects no light but only the strength and grace to accept this will, as it comes down the chain of command, with total obedience and blind faith. The new emphasis in the theology of the Church sees the Holy Spirit working *in the collective* and 'collegial' effort of all, each in his own sphere and according to his own function in the Church".[28]

Those who knew Thomas Merton very well recognized that they were faced with a complex personality, and his statements on various subjects sometimes tended to be contradictory at first glance. Monastic renewal was no exception, and in reading some of his remarks on the subject, one feels that there was a certain ambiguity which he himself failed to face squarely. For example, Merton spoke passionately of the need for renewal: "Renewal is something deeper and more total than reform. Reform was proper to the needs of the Church at the time of the Council of Trent, where the whole structure of religious life had collapsed, even though there was still a great deal of vitality among religious. Today the structure and organization is firm and intact: what is lacking is a deep and fruitful understanding of the real meaning of religious life".[29] He went on to define renewal as a restoration of authentic meaning to forms and acts that must recover their full value as sacred signs. Yet in a talk he gave to some rather conventional nuns in Calcutta shortly before his death, he deplored some trends in renewal in the United States, such as "a collapse of formal structures that were no longer properly understood; a repudiation of genuine tradition, discipline, contemplation, trivializing the monastic life".[30]

These are rather strong statements for a proponent of renewal in the monastic world. Again, one must consider the audience to whom he was addressing himself. Merton accommodated himself easily to his audience, and began where he found people. It is certainly true to say that his tone was quite different when speaking to a group of revolutionary students in Santa Barbara at the Center for the Study of Democratic Institutions.

It must be admitted that basically Thomas Merton was a man of tradition, which he knew well and loved. Yet, he was not a monk who believed in preserving the past for the sake of preservation. Perhaps only someone steeped in authentic monastic tradition as Merton was can really speak out meaningfully on the subject of monastic renewal. Needless to say, he did this without hesitation, but here he minces no words: "Certain structures need to be shaken, certain structures have to fall. We need not be revolutionaries within our institutions . . . . But on the other hand, we don't want to go to the other extreme and just simply be ostriches refusing to see

19

that these institutions are in many respects outdated, and that perhaps renewal may mean the collapse of some institutional structures and starting over again with a whole new form".[31]

Speaking of the spirit of openness to renewal in religious circles, which Merton considered most important in any renewal of religious life, he went on to say: "This means that observances which are 'closed' and incomprehensible' even to the religious themselves will almost inevitably generate a spirit of pretentiousness and artificiality which is incompatible with the true Gospel simplicity. Such observances must either be re-thought so that they recover a living meaning, or they must be discarded, and if necessary replaced by others that fulfill the function which they have ceased to fulfill".[32]

In studying the various statements made by Thomas Merton over the years on the subject of monastic renewal, one realizes that he was functioning as a critic, showing several sides of an issue, pointing out weaknesses on both sides of a question. This is apparent in dealing with the delicate subject of the monk's withdrawal from the world, his need for a certain *distance.* In the opening pages of *Contemplation in a World of Action,* Merton writes: "It is certainly true that this special perspective necessarily implies that the monk will be in some sense critical of the world, of its routines, its confusions, and its sometimes tragic failures to provide other men with lives that are fully sane and human. The monk can and must be open to the world, but at the same time he must be able to get along without a naive and uncritical 'secularity' which blandly assumes that everything in the world is at every moment getting better and better for everybody".[33] He admits this critical balance is often very difficult to achieve, but it is something the monk must strive for. "For the monastic life has a certain prophetic character about it: not that the monk should be able to tell what is about to happen in the Kingdom of God, but in the sense that he is a living witness to the freedom of the sons of God and to the essential difference

between that freedom and the spirit of the world".[34]

Merton was conscious of the fact that God so loved the world that he gave his only-begotten Son, but he also knew well that the Son of God came into a world that refused to receive him, a world that opposed and rejected him. Merton summed up his position in these moving words: "The monastic life then must maintain this prophetic seriousness, this wilderness perspective, this mistrust of any shallow optimism which overlooks the ambiguity and the potential tragedy of 'the world' in its response to the Word. And there is only one way for the monk to do this: to live as a man of God who has been manifestly 'called out of the world' to an existence that differs radically from that of other men, however sincere, however Christian, however holy, who have remained in the world".[35]

Dom Jean Leclercq in his excellent introduction to *Contemplation in a World of Action,* published after Merton's death, ends by quoting a letter from Thomas Merton which bears repeating here. In this letter accepting the invitation to come to Bangkok, Thailand, where he was to meet his death, Merton wrote to Leclercq: "The great problem for monasticism today is, 'not survival, but prophecy' ".[35] And those words are as true today as when they were written, a decade ago.

In his later years, Merton often compared the monk to the social critic, and as an example he pointed out that the earliest monks fled the secular society of the time and sought solitude and silence and purity of heart in the desert of Egypt. It was the monk's way of renouncing the culture of his day, and his withdrawal from society was his personal criticism of the world as he viewed it. In his address at Bangkok, a few hours before his death, Merton referred to a young French revolutionary student who had made the statement some weeks earlier at the Center for the Study of Democratic Institutions at Santa Barbara: "We are monks, too". Merton was deeply impressed by these words, and he reflected: "The monk is essentially someone who takes up a critical attitude toward the world and its structures, just as these students identify themselves as people who have taken up a critical attitude toward the contemporary world and its structures".[37] The criticism was quite different, as Merton pointed out. Yet he was saying something that was important for the monk to hear: "However, the student seemed to be alluding to the fact that if one is to call himself in some way or other a monk, he must have in some way or other reached some kind of critical conclusion about the validity of certain claims made by secular society and its structures with regard to the end of man's existence. In other words, the monk is somebody who says, in one way or another, that the claims of the world are fraudulent".[38]

In this respect Merton was closer to Karl Rahner and his "diaspora" Christian than to the over-enthusiastic optimism of some followers of Teilhard de Chardin. Reflections on the atrocities of the twentieth century, especially the "holocaust" of six and a half million Jews by the Nazis and our own ignominious performance in Vietnam, made him very much a sober realist; yet he remained a person of Christian hope in the ultimate victory of Christ, despite human shortcomings.

During the course of his Asian journey, Merton gave a number of talks: at the Temple of Understanding in Calcutta, to the Jesuit scholastics near Darjeeling, and of course his last conference at the meeting of Asian monastic leaders in Bangkok. Reading over these texts, some of which have been published as appendices to *The Asian Journal,* we see again the same balanced position between the extreme right and the reactionary left in renewal matters. Speaking of the irrelevance of monks in an informal talk in Calcutta, he asks the rhetorical question which he then proceeds to answer: "Are monks and hippies and poets relevant? No, we are deliberately irrelevant. We live with an ingrained irrelevance which is proper to every human being. The marginal man accepts the basic irrelevance of the human condition, an irrelevance which is manifested above all by the fact of death".[39]

Ironically, Merton then spoke of death and the marginal person, the monk, the displaced person, the prisoner, as a witness to life in these deeply moving words: "All these people live in the presence of death, which calls into question the meaning of life. He [the monk] struggles with the fact of death in himself, trying to seek something deeper than death; because there is something deeper than death, and the office of the monk or the marginal person, the meditative person or the poet is to go beyond death even in this life, to go beyond the dichotomy of life and death and to be, therefore, a witness to life".[40]

If anything can ultimately be said about Thomas Merton, it must be that he was "a witness to life". May his great spirit remain with us as we continue our renewal. In some sense the monastic life, like the Church itself, will always be renewing itself, and the wisdom and insights of Thomas Merton can assist us not only today, but especially in the years to come.

Brother Patrick Hart

Abbey of Gethsemani

Michael Casey

WITHIN A TRADITION
OF PRAYER

One aspect of Merton's approach to prayer which is often overlooked is the extent to which his viewpoint was colored by his years of immersion in the tradition of mainline Western monastic thought. Everybody knows of his interest in East Asian practices of meditation, especially toward the end of his life. Moreover, it is not always appreciated that this development was possible only within the context of values absorbed during a lifetime of reading and study in a climate which was typically and exclusively Western.

Merton's style is, in fact, deceptive. In both his books and his tapes he comes across as an easy-going and humorous man, who wrote in a language which was easy to understand and who rarely gives the impression of preaching down to his readers. In many ways he appeared as a personable figure, who seemed to know what he was talking about and had the ability to make contact with his readers and to be aware of their needs and aspirations. This sympathy generated by his early autobiography never really deserted him. For some reason, many men and women whose religious faith had long since gone underground and whose lives were far from monastic, seemed to find it easier to identify with this distant and solitary monk than with the flesh and blood representatives of religion in their own neighborhood. Yet even though Merton seemed to have the common touch, he was, in fact, something out of the ordinary and far from being a lightweight or a dabbler.

There was something different about Merton. Partly this stemmed from his own colorful background. His career was peppered with persons, places and events of sufficient interest to ensure that his autobiography was more than a mere chronicle of spiritual states. Beyond this was his own personality and temperament. His intensity, individualism and energy were such that would not permit him to melt into a crowd for long, even though there may have been times in which he tried to do just this. Finally there was the fact of effort. One of the things which saved Merton from becoming a talented spiritual eclectic on the academic fringe was the fact that he was prepared to commit himself to an unexciting institutional way of life and to operate within its parameters. Nobody survives within a fixed institutional setting without some friction or difficulty. But to be creative in such a context brings with it a degree of isolation, misunderstanding and frustration which requires proportionate effort and singlemindedness to overcome. That Merton was responsive to his talents and was able to live a productive and (it seems to me) predominantly happy life, indicates an exercise of willpower and an investment of energy which is, in some sense, belied by his casual and easy-going style. And if it is true that being Merton involved a lot of hard work, then it is probably also true that we who read his writings will fail to appreciate the full meaning of what he says unless we have some understanding of the implicit factors operative in the development of the very ideas and values which he expressed with such apparent facility.

There is current in some circles an interpretation of Merton's life which I believe to be as false as it is facile. According to this, Merton was more or less spiritually developed when he entered Gethsemani. In his early years there he resolutely resisted the sundry idiocies which passed for spirituality at that time, meanwhile propagating the essentials of his own through his writing, which was the only forum available to him. This lasted until such time as he was put into a position of formation in which it became possible for him to influence the development of others. As time went on he became more critical of the institutional Church and of its teaching. His interest in East Asian meditational writings is seen as the result of dissatisfaction with Christian fare, and his becoming a hermit is interpreted as another step toward dissociation from the Gethsemani community. Finally, "as everyone knows", he was really on the point of leaving altogether when Providence intervened in the form of faulty electrical wiring.

It is, undoubtedly, a good story and it would certainly make a good film. But, to anyone who knows even a little about the concrete realities of monastic life, such a fantastic farrago of fact and fiction has a credibility rating of almost zero. For someone with an axe to grind with the institutional Church, Merton becomes almost a martyr, a prophetic voice in a wilderness. Nothing is further from the truth. I think that history, if it is interested, will probably show that Merton was as much influenced by the monastic institution as influential within it. Without Gethsemani and the tradition of life and thought behind it, the Merton whom we know would probably never have emerged.

It is not possible to overestimate the influence which the experience of monastic life exercised on Merton's spiritual development. It was within the context of Western monastic life that the distant vision of contemplation gradually became concrete reality. This was so primarily because his membership of the monastic order provided him with routine access to the sources from which contemplative life springs. In the first place it was a support system for a life in which the instincts were reined. A sustained life of contemplation is impossible without a certain ordering of life, an acceptance of discipline and a willingness to be changed. Merton's belonging to Gethsemani offered him the possibility of a progressive liberation from the tyranny of a selfish life and this is of fundamental importance. Secondly, it meant that he was initiated into the practice of worship and invited to transcend himself in a form of prayer crafted by centuries of contemplative experience. No one who was exposed to the monolithic objectivity of the old liturgy could ever escape being conditioned by the roll of its Latin cadences and suffused by its aura of otherworldliness. The Latin office, in particular, was a real schooling in the sacred, and the spiritual formation it offered has proved to be durable. Thirdly, Merton could not but be profoundly changed by his experience of living with men who, according to their divers lights, were seeking the same goal as he. There was a massive facticity about monastic life at the time which readily impressed itself on the mind and heart of the monks; notwithstanding the rigorous standardization of observances there was a spiritual identity specific to each house which seemed to stay with a monk to his dying breath. I cannot gauge to what extent Merton thought of himself and was seen by others as a "Gethsemani man", but I am quite sure that the very fact of his spending so much of his life at Gethsemani must have resulted in a substantial shaping of his personal spirituality.

Merton's chronicled "temptations" all seem to have been purely domestic affairs. There seems to have been no question of his being urgently attracted to family life or to an active ministry, much less in the direction of wild living and unbelief. In other words, there can be no real doubt that he accepted the primary premise on which Cistercian life is based, the pursuit of a life of relatively intense prayer. His problems seem to have been more in the area of doubting whether the values which he accepted could be implemented in the Gethsemani community as he knew it.

In fact, this is not such an unusual difficulty, especially among perceptive and fervent younger monks. In large measure, the roots of the problem are to be sought not so much in the community's lack of zeal as in the monk's defective self-knowledge. It is often a case of what might be called monastic delusions of grandeur. For most people the solution lies in the direction of accepting that *no* social setting can ever be more than an approximate framework in fulfilling one's destiny. It is a skeleton which the individual is required to flesh out. A monastic community can point the way to a life of prayer and support the monk in his pursuit of it, but each person has finally to walk his own path and at his own pace, restraining his impatience when the going is good, not losing his nerve when things start to go wrong. Part of the acceptance of the community, notwithstanding its limitations, is the readiness to listen to others and to accept their judgment regarding what seems to be an appropriate next step. Sometimes this is relatively straightforward. But often, especially in times of personal confusion, the fact that others might have an alternative viewpoint about the ordering of one's life appears as a monstrous imposition. The acceptance of a Providence which runs counter to one's own projects is always a test of faith, but it is certainly not unusual. The prolonged and often painful process of coming to grips with this dilemma and the consequent necessity of re-defining one's self-image and sense of vocation in terms of it, form a regular part of the purification which preceded a person's transition into contemplative prayer. "Certain temptations and delusions are to be regarded as a normal part of the life of prayer".[1] Merton's difficulties probably differ from those of many of his contemporaries only in the fact of their being public knowledge.

Merton was certainly not alone in his dissatisfaction with the sugar-coated work ethic which prevailed in many monasteries at that time, though perhaps it pained him more. There was a certain duplicity apparent in those houses which proclaimed an undying desire for contemplative prayer and yet denied their monks the leisure and formation necessary to make this desire a reality. The emphasis on doing without and living hard was no substitute for a personalized induction into the life of prayer. Of those who survived this sort of crisis we find several whose solution was found as much in the library as in the church. So long as they had a position in which at least some time was available for substantial reading, it became possible for them to supply for the defects in their own formation through a personal labor of reading. I believe that Thomas Merton was such a one.

One of the characteristic strengths of Benedictine monasticism is the importance it attributes to substantial and sustained reading. According to an ancient axiom "a monastery without a library is like an army camp without an arsenal" *(Claustrum sine armario quasi castrum sine armentario)*. While it is always possible for this zeal to degenerate either into the mindless repetition of somebody else's devotional thoughts or into a minute pursuit of erudite trivia, the capacity to read for profit is the characteristic requirement for the Western monk. The real purpose of such *lectio divina* and study is the development of those skills necessary to enable the monk to distill from the ancient writings, beliefs and values which throw light on his own individual and communal existence and which can serve as an animating principle of behavior. A monk reads to find wisdom. It is especially through such prayerful reading that a monk's consciousness is transformed and through this change is born not only a personal vision but also a distinctive style of fulfilling his vocation. A monk feels at home in a monastery only to the extent that he has arrived at an appreciation of his own spiritual identity, and this is why, in the Benedictine tradition, serious reading plays an important role in the settling of vocations.

Merton read much. Understanding this is the key to comprehending how he managed to survive within the restrictive confines of Cistercian life at that time. To a large extent it was through reading that he was enabled to find and formulate a system of meaning for himself and to have something over to fill his books and lectures. I have not seen an exhaustive discussion of Merton's reading habits, but it is fairly obvious that he read widely and retained much of what he read. In the material he prepared for his students he revealed a competent and detailed acquaintance with monastic tradition which was quite unusual in those days. He was fortunate in having the languages to give him contact with both primary and secondary sources and he had the interest and the diligence to pursue paths that were somewhat off the beaten track. What is apparently his last book on prayer, *The Climate of Monastic Prayer* (also published as *Contemplative Prayer*), in which we find an astonishing interplay of monastic and other sources, gives some idea of the extent to which he externalized and re-expressed the thoughts of others.

What I aim to do in the rest of this article is to comment briefly on a number of themes which are important in Merton's conception of prayer and to relate them with what I consider to be their fundamental source, classical Western monastic tradition. This is not to deny that Merton had other sources or that he himself may have contributed something original. It is simply to point out that Merton, far from growing out of traditional monasticism, from one point of view seems to have been growing into it.

Anthropological Basis

"It is this sound anthropological foundation to Merton's theology of prayer, that principally heightens the originality of his teaching". So writes Father Higgins in his treatment of Merton's theology of prayer.[2] There is, however, a real difference between what is characteristic and what is original. Merton's characteristic view of human reality is not his own creation. It is a restatement of the traditional Christian anthropology found already in Augustine and Gregory of Nyssa and popularized within the Christian tradition by Bernard of Clairvaux & other writers of his generation.

This traditional teaching on the nature of man centers

around the biblical statement that man was made as "the image of God" (Gen 1: 26-27). The principal content of such an emphasis was the affirmation that between God and man there is a natural, pre-elective affinity. Man is endowed with an innate capacity for God. When a person seeks God, he is simply responding to the deepest imperative of his being. He is being himself, not contriving to force himself into some mould of being substantially alien to his nature. On the other hand, to eliminate the search for God from one's conscious life is to initiate a sequence of steps whose ultimate effect is dehumanization. Man eventually destroys himself when he denies God. The starting point of all monastic spirituality is the understanding that man is made for union with God and the affirmation that the life of prayer is the natural outcome of mature and healthy human being.

Merton certainly had this conviction, and the terms in which he expressed himself of it were often direct drawings from the concepts and language of monastic tradition. To some extent, his whole life can be seen as a parable proclaiming the primacy of the spiritual. His most basic social criticism was that Western culture overlooked and undervalued man's deep spiritual potential, and as a result relegated religion to the status of an optional extra. It made spiritual values peripheral to the central business of making money and exercising power. His occasional criticism of the Church and of religious communities are regularly provoked by the infiltration into these bodies of worldly values and the practical disregard for the human centrality of contemplation. Later, when his powerful irony was levelled at other dehumanizing factors in society, materialism, acquisitiveness, racism, violence and so forth, the unstated presupposition is the same. Man was made for God, concentration on subordinate pursuits distorts the person and causes his spiritual sensitivity and creativity to atrophy. A society based on material values will certainly destroy itself. The same theme dominates nearly all his writings, and although it is stated with a unique passion and is bound closely to

[margin note: religion is not optional extra, but essential !*]*

movements in the contemporary world, it remains a familiar theme throughout the history of spirituality. It is a conviction which no reader of monastic sources can escape, and there can be no doubt that Merton's contact with the great minds of the Western monastic past helped him to clarify his stance and to express it verbally.

Silence in Prayer

As a young man Merton wrote sickeningly about silence as a specifically "Trappist" institution. The tone of his eulogies was romantic and superficial, and their total effect was almost certainly baneful. At this early stage of his monastic career, the emphasis seems to have been on internalizing the organizational form of silence and so arriving at some form of inward peace, far from the noise and tumult of secular society, and free from the clangor of a technological world with which he, personally, seems to have had little affinity. As far as one can judge, a more mature appreciation of the role of silence in the life of prayer came only later.

Emphasis on stillness and quiet in prayer flows from an appreciation of the innate spiritual capacity of human being. An appreciation of silence is impossible without an alternative anthropology. Prayer does not have to be added on to human being from outside by the performance of certain acts and the saying of appropriate words. It is something that comes naturally to man. It emerges from within, but on one condition. It requires a certain disengagement from external activities. Silence in prayer is not the pious somnolence of one too lazy to make an effort—Merton remained an intransigent opponent of Quietism throughout his life—but it is the necessary condition of alertness and responsiveness which is required if a person is to come under the influence of grace. Such a recession from external involvement and from the tumult of words and thoughts is, perhaps, the ultimate exercise in selflessness, since it involves the renunciation of all independent operation so that the person may be totally at the behest of the indwelling Word.

This sort of silence is constantly recommended in monastic treatises on prayer, where feelingfulness and concentration are consistently preferred to talkativeness and the dispersal of energies.[3] There is, in the monastic approach to personal prayer, a sort of reverence which corresponds closely to *apophasis* in theological discourse. A necessary part of monastic prayer is the acceptance of the transcendent character of the divine mystery which is expressed in the preference for humility and quiet over drama, self-expression or conceptual clarity.

Merton was clearly part of this tradition. In particular he recognized and inveighed against some specific modern tendencies which militate against this faith-filled silence. One of the dangers recognized as confronting many of our contemporaries was that of coming to prayer with a consumer-society mentality.[4] He was aware that many people cannot find silence in prayer simply because they are wracked with a spiritual acquisitiveness which will not permit them to be at peace until they have attained to some specific and pleasurable spiritual experience which is the goal underlying all their efforts. Such a restless search for spiritual "highs" is as destructive of the expectant stillness required for contemplation as relentless ratiocination or unbridled chattering. It consistently results in a disappointing dryness when the person's efforts yield a different result. Merton often spoke out against this tendency, combining in his statements a traditional concern for silence in prayer with an incisive perception of the temper of the times.

> *The Cloud (of Unknowing),* like all the great documents in the apophatic tradition, warns us that the appetite for experiences—or, more crudely, for kicks— is the greatest danger to the development of an authentic mystical life.[5]

Self-knowledge

Merton was one with the medieval Cistercian authors in

underlying the crucial importance of self-knowledge in the
process of growing into contemplation. Genuine prayer, he
re-iterated, cannot co-exist with comfortable delusions, lax
living and a tendency toward narcissism in the spiritual life.
The desire for God feeds on an awareness of one's own
nothingness, on one's pressing need for the divine mercy and
the recognition of one's status before God as that of a sinner—a
real sinner, not merely one who affects the title for politeness'
sake. Complacency in the spiritual pursuit is a result of mental
slackness. It is a subterfuge by which a person excuses himself
from much effort by refusing to look very closely at the reality
of his own life. Its only antidote is purity of heart, which is the
monastic term for a certain keenness of the inward eye, a sharp-
ness of spiritual vision which is in direct proportion to a person's singlemindedness in pursuing the Good.

> In the language of the monastic fathers, all prayer,
> reading, and all the activities of the monastic life are
> aimed at *purity of heart,* an unconditional and
> totally humble surrender to God, a total acceptance
> of ourselves and of our situation as willed by him. It
> means the renunciation of all deluded images of our-
> selves, all exaggerated estimates of our own capa-
> cities, in order to obey God's will as it comes to us in
> the difficult demands of life in its exacting truth . . .
> Purity of heart is the enlightened awareness of the
> new man, as opposed to the complex and perhaps
> rather disreputable fantasies of the "old man".[6]

We find throughout Merton's writings a constant return to
the theme of humility, truth and the acceptance of one's own
weakness. He seems to have had little patience with the pretentiousness and pompousness of many professional religious
persons. His works are not without a twinkling of that irony
which has long been the mainstay of monastic humor, though
behind the amusement perhaps there was some anger at those

who used religion to advance the cause of *bourgeois* respectability.

Negative Experience

Many readers of *The Climate of Monastic Prayer* professed themselves puzzled at its heavy emphasis on the notion of "dread". Although it is obvious that Merton's formulation of this theme owes much to the existentialist thought of the last generation, the theme itself is fundamentally traditional. The fact for which many are unprepared is that the ascent to truth is accomplished not through pleasant advances in wisdom and insight, but through the painful unlayering of levels of falsehood. It is not so much a process of enrichment and accumulation as a matter of being progressively purified and despoiled of prejudices and delusions which cling more tightly than a second skin.

In Merton's view, it was through the painful experience of dread that a person arrived at a degree of self-knowledge on which contemplation could be built. To seek to avoid the pain of being emancipated from the inhibiting patterns of thought and behavior which characterize a "worldly" existence is to preclude the possibility of an authentic growth in prayerfulness.

> It is precisely the function of dread to break down this glass house of false interiority and to deliver man from it. It is dread, and dread alone, that drives a man out of this private sanctuary in which his solitude becomes horrible to himself without God. But without dread, without the disquieting capacity to see and to repudiate the idolatry of devout ideas and imaginings, man would remain content with himself and with his "inner life" in meditation, in liturgy or in both. Without dread, the Christian cannot be delivered from the smug self-assurance of the devout ones who know all the answers to advance, who

possesses all the *clichés* of the inner life and can defend themselves with infallible ritual forms against every risk and every demand of dialogue with human need and human desperation.[7]

The events in life which precipitate this realization of individual inadequacy take many forms and are tailored to the person's own biography. Among the more usual can be enumerated a growing distaste for prayer, unsettlement with regard to vocation, personal failure—often in the sexual sphere, friction with individuals or administrators in one's community, difficulties with work or studies. On top of these patent problems is the anxiety which they produce and the behavioral oddities which often result from an effort to reduce that tension. The only way out of such a painful impasse is the recognition of the unsaved reality of one's independent selfhood and the courageous decision not to attempt to evade the dread which such a recognition evokes. It is only through such an acceptance that a person allows God entry into his life precisely as Savior and Dispenser of mercy. So long as one remains self-satisfied and secure, the God of mercy keeps his distance.

Negative experience has the effect of increasing one's dependence on God and, as such, it progressively liberates one from dependence on external gratifications. As a person develops in prayer his life becomes simpler and he himself is content with less. Indeed, as Merton frequently notes, there eventuates a certain preference for the desert with its starkness and lack of novelty and less than total light. There is no formula which can suddenly transmute such negative components of experience into interesting and pleasurable happenings. What has to change is not the diet but the digestion. A person who is beginning to find God finds himself adapting to the conditions with which God surrounds himself. Because he becomes progressively more satisfied with little he becomes proportionately happier. His joy comes to be no longer based on factors external to himself but on his own renunciation of the pursuit of pleasure, and as such becomes something relatively permanent and not easily destroyed.

Prayer of the Heart

Reacting strongly against the rationalistic spirituality which had penetrated nearly all corners of the Church's life when he was a young monk, Merton experienced a profound attraction toward the ancient monastic insistence on the *heart* as the site of prayer. As one sensitive to beauty and a poet of some talent, he must have had an intuitive awareness that the source of human creativity and verve lies deeper than consciousness, that it was not through the exercise of rational powers or the faculty of will that man attains the absolute, but through the expansion of the human spirit. There is a certain amount of evidence to indicate that he understood the whole process of asceticism and discipline and the progressive purification accomplished through prayer as being the building up of a personal working relationship with one's own creative center. Merton's whole approach to prayer is based on the assumption that there is within the human person a region of interiority which is far removed from the zone of empirical experience. The monk's work is to seek his heart. It is to penetrate to this secret place, to encounter God there and to allow his influence to radiate from the heart into all areas of thought and conduct.

Merton's description of the heart fluctuates somewhat between theology, pop psychology and straight spiritual exhortation. Three characteristic quotations can, perhaps, indicate the direction of his thought.

The first comes from *The Climate of Monastic Prayer.*

> The concept of "the heart" might well be analyzed here. It refers to the deepest psychological ground of one's personality, the inner sanctuary where self-awareness goes beyond analytical reflection and opens one out into metaphysical and theological confrontation with the Abyss of the unknown yet

present—one who is "more intimate to us than we are to ourselves".[8]

The second comes from his essay on "Promethean Theology" in *The New Man.*

> Grace is given us for the precise purpose of enabling us to discover and actualize our deepest and truest self. Unless we discover this deep self we will never really know ourselves as persons. Nor will we know God. For it is by the door of this deep self that we enter into the spiritual knowledge of God. (And indeed, if we seek our true selves it is not in order to contemplate ourselves, but to pass beyond ourselves and find Him.)[9]

The third extract is taken from Merton's unpublished manuscript, *The Inner Experience,* some of which is reproduced in Raymond Bailey's informed discussion of Merton on mysticism.

> The inner self is as secret as God and, like him, it evades every concept that tries to seize hold of it with full possession. It is a life that cannot be held and studied as an object, because it is not "a thing". It is not reached and coaxed from hiding by any process under the sun, including meditation. All that we can do with any spiritual discipline is produce within ourselves something of the silence, the humility, the detachment, the purity of heart and the indifference which are required if the inner self is to make some shy, unpredictable manifestation of his *(sic)* presence.[10]

Monastic tradition repeatedly avers that man was made for union with God and that the dynamic energies which

39

propel man in God's direction are not to be found on the level of human ingenuity, enthusiasm, effort or activity. They result from the gift of grace. To avail himself of them, a person must accept the inevitability of a certain recession from external involvement. It is this same conviction which is behind a great deal of what Merton wrote on prayer.

Indifference to Techniques

We find in the books and articles written by Merton very few concrete directions for the practice of prayer. In fact, there are some indications that the last thing that he wanted to do was give the impression that a particular technique or practice was an infallible means of "getting contemplation", or that any particular method was so significant that it could not be bypassed. There is, in Merton's approach, a characteristic broadness which is a recognized feature of the monastic tradition of prayer. There is an acceptance of the fact that different things work for different people and a recognition that an individual changes, so that what may be suitable for him at one stage of his life may be entirely unsatisfactory at other times. A person has no alternative but to respond to the real setting in which he finds himself, with the result that his prayer is necessarily fabricated from the various inner and outward components of his life. It is not something superimposed on an already complete life; it is the specifically spiritual response which animates and unifies the disparate features of a unique and concrete human existence. It draws upon whatever resources happen to be available while compensating for elements which unavoidably inhibit or restrict. Prayer grows out of life. Merton's teaching is, at this point, in complete accord with Western monastic principles. Fixed slots for prayer and complicated methods of meditation find rare exponents in authentic monastic sources. On the contrary, monks find it difficult to talk about prayer without saying something about the quality of life as a whole. Prayer is not an isolated department of life, it is the realization of the God-ward potential inherent in every life.

40

Granted this fundamental reservation about techniques, Merton often mentions the possibility of using short scriptural texts as a basis for prayer. His references to the Eastern practice of the "Jesus Prayer" are frequent and favorable. But there is no trace of rigidity here. It is a common experience that as a person reads the Scriptures or sings the Psalms he often discovers formulas of prayer which seem to echo the unspoken aspirations of his heart. It is useful for a person to keep an eye out for such texts for they can often lubricate his periods of personal prayer. It is not a high-powered process; it is simply a matter of his quietly repeating the texts and savoring them for as long as the attraction remains. If there is any monastic method of prayer, this is it. But it is a flexible process which supports prayer without quenching its naturalness or appearing contrived and at odds with the ordinary levels of daily living.

A second reason for a certain reservation about techniques is the fear that they may become means by which a person insulates himself against God, protecting himself from God's action and short-circuiting any emergent movement of purification. What has already been said about Merton's emphasis on the role of "dread" bears on this. Part of the means by which a person grows in prayerfulness is his acceptance of the experience of his own nothingness and the negativity with which his being is riddled. A method of prayer that is too "infallible" may well prevent his facing the fact that, of ourselves, we do not know how to pray as we ought. It may so fill the time of prayer that the felt need for God is extinguished.

The Implicit Support-system

Like the author of *The Cloud of Unknowing*, when Merton writes about prayer, he often does so taking for granted a whole range of values whose obviousness to him precludes their being mentioned. As a result, both authors are sometimes considered to be less specifically Christian and Catholic than they actually were. This is especially so when their works are read by non-believers.

41

The fact of Merton's living in an organized Catholic monastic community inevitably involved his being exposed to the whole spectrum of liturgical and devotional attitudes and practices, some of which he would have internalized and probably maintained throughout his life, though without ever placing particular emphasis on them.

> It is understood that the personal prayer of the monk is embedded in a life of psalmody, liturgical celebration and the meditative reading of Scripture (*lectio divina*). All this has both a personal and communal dimension.[11]

I think that it is entirely likely that many monks of an older age-bracket who did not know Merton personally, failed to understand that when he wrote of contemplation he did so from a standpoint which included liturgical participation, personal reading, devotion to Our Lady, acceptance of the Creed, fraternal charity and so forth. When they dismissed his writings, as many seem to have done, it was because his emphasis on "contemplation" appeared to them as too brash and too blatant, and too little rooted in a humble life of "ordinary prayer" and service. This is why some insistence on this point is necessary.

Merton's writings were not intended to promote a disembodied search for contemplation as an end in itself, but to bring out the contemplative dimension implicit in many devoted Christians' lives. He affirmed, together with the whole of monastic tradition, that the search for authentic prayer uses as its fundamental raw material the everyday components of a life of faith. What is different in the case of one who finds contemplation is not the range of ingredients, but the end result.

Broadness of Vision

Mention has already been made of the fact that even after entering the monastery, Merton continued to expand his own intellectual horizons. As a reader he seems to have ranged far and wide in his choice of books. From all accounts, his friends and contacts increased the scope of his interests and his emergence as something of a social critic gave further testimony to the fact that, although he lived apart from the world, he nevertheless considered its destiny closely linked with his own.

There is nothing narrow about Merton. It is pertinent to note that such broadness of vision is entirely characteristic of other great figures within Western monasticism. This is true not only of prominent personages such as Bernard and Bede, but also of the numberless army of monks whose lives remained unspectacular. As far as I am aware, this catholicity of interests is not very typical either of Eastern Christian monks or of the monks following the other great traditions of religious life throughout Asia. The catalogues of manuscripts copied and kept in medieval monasteries throughout Europe, attest the overriding humanity of those monks, just as the dispersal and destruction of such tomes by the forces of secularism must surely say something of the narrowing impact of such a philosophy.

Merton's humanity meant that he was open to wide-ranging influences, and because of this he was more liable to be emancipated from the narrowing effect of ideology and closed thinking. It is his ability to profit from what all sorts of people have to contribute that makes his writings good and enriching reading. They have something new to contribute. It is not a mere mindless juxtaposition of a jumble of elements from an assortment of sources. There is a real harmony in what he writes, deriving from his ability to integrate ideas coming from different traditions within the unity of his own experience and understanding. Perhaps he is a good example of the sort of monastic teacher envisaged by St Benedict, who was able to bring out from his storehouse, new things and old.

It is probably true to say that Merton read more widely than is usual, even for Western monks, but the fact that he was able to absorb into his own commanding vision much of what he encountered indicates that he was in accord with the ideals and practices of authentic Benedictinism throughout the centuries.

Opening to the East

Merton's progressive absorption in Eastern writings is part of this program. Anyone who lives a monastic life necessarily assimilates something of the philosophy which is its soul. Once a monk begins delving into monastic sources, he initiates what might be called a "journey to the East".

Christian monasticism began in the East and throughout its history it has flourished when it kept this contact alive. In the last chapter of the *Rule* of Saint Benedict, the monk who wishes a more profound understanding of his vocation is exhorted to return to the Scriptures and to the Fathers, and, in particular, to Basil and the tradition of the desert represented by Cassian. The twelfth century which was a period of unparalleled monastic renewal was simultaneously a time of resurgence of interest in the writings of the Christian East. Abbot Bamberger goes so far as to assert that it was precisely through his study of the Cistercians of the twelfth century that Merton's enthusiasm for the Greek Fathers was given impetus.[12] From the study of the monastic writings and such great figures as Gregory of Nyssa, his interest developed in the direction of Orthodoxy and particularly toward the representatives of the Russian monastic tradition.

From Eastern Christianity to the mystical and monastic strands in the other world religions is, perhaps, a considerable step. However in the case of somebody like Merton, who has already displayed an athletic interest in alternative formulations of the monastic ideal, it is not surprising. There is not much precedent for this sort of thing, but there are plenty of Western monks whose attention has been independently seized by the religious traditions of East Asia. It is, in fact, nothing more than an extension of the classical monastic interest in the East in an age where men and monks are far more fully aware of the existence of such traditions and have relatively easy access to their sources. There is a world of difference between an amateur eclectic producing his own blend of undigested doctrines and a mature monk with a vigorous contemplative life seeking alternative formulations of what he already possesses. Merton's interest in East Asian meditational techniques was not the result of disgust with traditional Christian teaching, nor was it a mindless meander through the spiritual supermarket. It was the natural outcome of an active and resourceful intelligence seeking a broader understanding of the experience of contemplative life.

The Contemplative Life

Merton's earlier writings on the contemplative life seem all to be marred by the defensiveness and triumphalism noticeable among most other apologists of that period. By the 60s something had changed. There was now a note of challenge to be detected in the words he addressed to contemplatives. There can be no doubt that he continued to appreciate the value of setting up religious communities with the primary purpose of imparting to their members the wisdom necessary to advance a life of contemplation. But he was voicing his dissatisfaction with the distortions and deviations which can thrive in such institutions once the animating vision is lost. He is often ironic about some of the things he either saw around him or heard about, but his mordant criticisms are not denials of the worthiness of the ideals in themselves, but demands that obstacles to the realization of such ideals be removed. He refused to accept the assumption that the monastic environment is intended to be a secure refuge for those who cannot cope with the realities of life and he scoffed at monasteries which tried to be a microcosmic reproduction of the patterns of thought and domination which are the ruin of society. His idea of contemplative life was, if anything, too idealistic. He demanded that monasteries be so singlemindedly oriented toward contemplation that sometimes one may wonder whether he really intended his words to be taken literally. One thing is certain. He never thought that contemplative orders should

45

be *less* contemplative.

The contemplative life demands a setting in which a person undertakes a sustained, unexciting and laborious pursuit of values which are largely foreign to our society and are continually demanding sacrifice of the individual. Without some sort of constant turning away from oneself in heartfelt conversion, this life becomes prone to degeneration. Observances become a parody, nothing more than a pattern of bizarrely disguised attempts at self-gratification, characterized by closed minds, fixed habits of behavior, and an intransigent and instinctive preference for the superficial. In his essay on "Openness and Cloister", he boldly tackled one of the features of contemporary contemplative life which seemed to him most likely to change in the climate of post-Vatican II renewal.[13] In it he clearly spoke of the narrowing effect of the present practice of enclosure on the minds and hearts of those who aspired to open themselves to contemplative prayer. It was an article much discussed at the time of its first appearance though not many communities really took to heart what he was driving at.

Toward the end of his life it became clear that Merton had lost his defensiveness about the contemplative life and felt secure enough to point to deficiencies in the practical pursuit of that goal. There seems to be a certain amount of evidence to the fact that he feared that in many cases contemplative life was being eroded by a new narrowness. The tenacity of traditionalism had been replaced with the tyranny of keeping up with fashions in religious living. In both cases the problem was the same; it was the overlooking of the "one thing necessary" and excessive submersion of individuals in the business of daily living. I imagine that to escape from the pointlessness of such pedestrian preoccupations must have been one of the attractions of becoming a hermit.

* * *

In this article I have tried to argue that Merton's most characteristic thoughts on the subject of prayer are completely in accord with the Western monastic tradition of prayer into which he was initiated at Gethsemani and in which he revelled until the end. I have not mentioned the pervasive presence of Saint John of the Cross nor the influence exercised by the English and Rhenish mystics. The whole question of sources demands a more exhaustive study than is possible here. But when it comes to the final analysis I am convinced that it will be impossible accurately to gauge the ebb and flow of influence without being immersed in the tradition of prayer typical of Western monasticism at its best.

Joseph Chu-Công

THE FAR EAST

It gives me joy to respond to the invitation to write something on Thomas Merton for Asian readers. Along with a dozen Cistercian novice masters of the American Region I was privileged to visit Thomas Merton and listen to him in his hermitage just a few months before he started out on his Asian journey in late 1968.

Merton was well known to the Asians. Many of his books have been translated into different Asian languages. For example, *Seeds of Contemplation* into Chinese; *The New Man, Life and Holiness, Seeds of Contemplation, Thoughts in Solitude, The Seven Storey Mountain, Basic Principles of Monastic Spirituality,* into Japanese. *Life and Holiness,* into Korean; and both *Seeds of Contemplation* and *No Man Is an Island* into Vietnamese, etc.[1]

In the following paragraphs I offer some observations on Merton's dialogue with a Zen scholar and teacher, Dr Daisetz Teitaro Suzuki, on the subject of wisdom. My remarks are mainly directed toward my fellow Asians, but I trust they will be of interest to Western readers as well, particularly those who are engaging in East–West dialogue today. First, a few words on Dr Suzuki.

The knowledge and practice of a spiritual way of life known as Ch'an or Zen has proved its worth during fifteen hundred years of application in China, Japan, Korea, Viet-Nam, and many other countries in the Far East. Zen Buddhism and almost all that is known of it in the West comes from the many books and lectures by the late D. T. Suzuki. Suzuki devoted his life to making the history and nature of Zen Buddhism known to the West. Christmas Humphreys, a friend and associate of D. T. Suzuki, wrote:

> It may be that in the days to come the mind of the West will be less prone to place in closed compartments in the inter-related functions of metaphysics and physics, mysticism and biology, psychology and religion, art and technology. Perhaps the religion of the future, in the sense of a personal attainment of direct experience of Reality, the awareness of a total man in a total universe, is already born. If it grows to manhood the name of one of its godfathers should be warmly remembered, that of D. T. Suzuki.[2]

D. T. Suzuki, who died in 1966 at the age of 95, was a remarkable figure in the field of Oriental philosophy, for he was at the same time a scholar of international rank, and a spiritual teacher who had himself attained the enlightenment he strove to hand on to others. In 1897 D. T. Suzuki came to the United States where he spent the following eleven years with only occasional visits to Europe. In 1911 he married an American wife, Mrs Beatrice Lane Suzuki, a noted scholar in Shington Buddhism.

Merton knew D. T. Suzuki's work, corresponded with him, and published a short dialogue in conjunction with him which

Merton entitled *Wisdom in Emptiness*. During Suzuki's last trip to the United States a few years before he died, Merton was able to speak with him on two occasions. Later Merton wrote of D. T. Suzuki:

> I had the great privilege and pleasure of meeting him. One had to meet this man in order fully to appreciate him. He seemed to me to embody all the indefinable qualities of the "Superior Man" of the ancient Asian, Taoist, Confucian and Buddhist traditions, or rather in meeting him one seemed to meet that "True Man of No Title"[3] that Chuang-Tzu and the Zen Masters speak of. And of course this is the man one really wants to meet. Who else is there?
>
> In meeting Dr Suzuki and drinking a cup of tea with him I felt I had met this one Man. It was like finally arriving at one's own home. A very happy experience, to say the least. One cannot understand Buddhism until one meets it in this existential manner in a person in whom it is alive. Then there is no longer a problem of understanding doctrines which cannot help being a bit exotic for a Westerner, but only a question of appreciating this value which is self-evident. I am sure that no alert and intelligent Westerner ever met Dr Suzuki without something of the same experience.[4]

Merton saw many similarities between the Desert Fathers' austere spirituality and Zen simplicity, between the *Verba Seniorum* and the *Sayings* of the Zen Masters. In 1959 after Merton completed his translation from the Latin of some one hundred and fifty sayings of the Desert Fathers (which Merton entitled *Wisdom of the Desert*), he sent the text to Dr Suzuki with the request that a dialogue on the "Wisdom" of the Desert Fathers and the Zen Masters be opened. Merton wrote:

> In the spring of 1959, after the completion of some translations from the *Verba Seniorum,* which has been published by New Directions under the title of *The Wisdom of the Desert,* it was decided to send the translation to Daisetz T. Suzuki, one of the prominent Oriental scholars and contemplatives of our day . . . He received with pleasure the suggestions to engage in a dialogue about the "Wisdom" of the Desert Fathers and of the Zen Masters.[5]

The dialogue is composed of (i) Merton's copy of the text of *The Wisdom of The Desert* to D. T. Suzuki, (ii) Suzuki's reply in the form of an essay entitled *Knowledge and Innocence,* (iii) Merton's response to Suzuki with an essay entitled *The Recovery of Paradise,* (iv) Suzuki's final remarks, and lastly (v) Merton's last words. I do not intend to harmonize the teaching of Merton with that of D. T. Suzuki, nor do I mean to put one against the other. I intend only to search out the underlying, or "above dwelling" wisdom with which the two great men are concerned.

Thomas Merton: Wisdom as the Quest for Salvation

Merton's vision of the "Wisdom of the Desert" can be summarized in one phrase—the quest for salvation. He wrote:

> In the fourth century A.D. the deserts of Egypt, Palestine, Arabia and Persia were peopled by a race of men who have left behind them a strange reputation. They were the first Christian hermits, who abandoned the cities of the pagan world to live in solitude. Why did they do this? The reasons were many and various, but they can all be summed up in one word as the quest for "salvation".[6]

Merton went on to explain this "quest for salvation" by saying that

The Fathers sought most of all their true self, in Christ. And in order to do this, they had rejected completely the false self, fabricated under social compulsion in "the world". He (the Desert Father) could not retain the slightest identification with his superficial, transient, self-constructed self, He had to lose himself in the inner, hidden reality of a self that was transcendent, mysterious, half-known, and lost in Christ. He had to die to the values of transient existence as Christ died to them on the Cross, and rise from the dead with Him in the light of an entirely new wisdom.[7]

Merton's notion of wisdom as "the quest for salvation" or "the search for the true self" and "the dying and rising with Christ" could have induced D. T. Suzuki to engage in a lively dialogue on "vertical", or "transcendental" wisdom (in Sanscrit: Prajna), which is enlightenment. But Merton elaborated on these ideas during his lengthy *Introduction* in which he also touched on social, moral, and even political issues.

Daisetz T. Suzuki: Wisdom as Emptiness or Innocence
D. T. Suzuki, like any Zen-man, distinguishes between horizontal and vertical wisdom. Horizontal wisdom leads to knowledge *about* things. It is common in human learning and thinking for us to reach a certain level of knowledge, and then go on expanding that level. It is said that in Zen practice the aim is not to elaborate but to penetrate, that is to say, to taste the vertical wisdom.

Vertical wisdom is that penetrating insight which leads to knowing things as they are. It goes upward, as it were, to the higher understanding and realization of truth. Vertical wisdom is also called "transcendental wisdom", transcendental in the sense of transcending or going beyond the mere knowledge of things. It is knowing or awareness *as such,* beyond the duality of subject and object, which is the realm of philosophy.

Transcendental wisdom is knowing, knowing, knowing; that is to say, subject, predicate, and object all being the same. D. T. Suzuki wrote about the working out of transcendental wisdom, or Prajna, this way:

> Conceptually, Prajna makes its first movements towards the apprehension of what it supposes its object. When it is actually taken hold of, however, the seizer and the seized become one; dualism ceases and there is a state of perfect identity which is known as enlightenment, and also all-knowledge. This experience may be described in this way too: Prajna first divides or contradicts itself in order to see itself, starting a state of duality such as means and end, subject and object, this and that, the seer and the seen. When the work of seeing itself is accomplished, in Prajna there is no more duality. Prajna is seen in enlightenment, and enlightenment in Prajna. It sees everywhere its own names, only differently spelt.[8]

Suzuki understood wisdom in this vertical or transcendental sense. For him, to be wise is to know things in their Suchness. It is to know things as they are in themselves. It is enlightenment. He wrote:

> Enlightenment is another term for Suchness, or Emptiness. Enlightenment is described in the Mahaprajnaparamita in the following terms: by enlightenment is meant emptiness, suchness, reality-limit, spiritual realm, and essence. Enlightenment itself is the highest and ultimate reality; it is the norm not subject to change; it is indestructible, beyond discrimination; it is true, pure, and all-pervading knowledge possessed by all the Buddhas; it is the most fundamental perfection whereby the Buddhas gain an insight into the nature of all realities, of all forms, it

Cf to Eckhart!

54

is beyond every mode of expression, beyond all thought construction created by the mind.

This Suchness, or "Emptiness" as a form of wisdom is often found in the thinking of primitive cultures such as the Eskimos. Dr H. Ostermann, in his report of the Fifth Thule Expedition, wrote about an Eskimo named Najagneg, who experienced the presence of what he called "The Man of Ten-Horse-Power". When asked if he believed in any of the power he spoke of, he answered:

> Yes, a power that we call Sila, one that cannot be explained in so many words. A strong spirit, the upholder of the universe, of the weather, in fact all life on earth so mighty that his speech to man comes not through ordinary words, but through storms, snowfall, rain showers, the tempest of the sea, through all the forces that man fears, or through sunshine, calm seas, or small, innocent, playing children who understand nothing. When times are good. Sila has nothing to say to mankind. He has disappeared into his infinite nothingness and remains away as long as people do not abuse life, but have respect for their daily food. No one has ever seen Sila. His place of sojourn is so mysterious that he is with us and infinitely far away at the same time.[9]

For Suzuki, as for all Zen Masters, *Suchness* is what a thing is, the nature of a thing. To reach the *Suchness* of a thing is to attain supreme knowledge, or ultimate wisdom. Ernest Wood asserted that: "If the term God, divested of all anthropomorphism, is used for the original power of self-being or self nature, then the Eastern view has always been that man can know God by overcoming the impurity which one's mind imposes on his seeing."[10]

This is the kind of wisdom with which Suzuki intended to

enter into dialogue with Merton. Suzuki has difficulty dealing with the Cross of Christ mentioned by Merton in the Introduction to *The Wisdom of the Desert*. But he accepted fully the notion of Christ as the One who said, "Before Abraham was, I am" (John 8: 58), that is to say, the eternal Christ.[11] About the Crucified Christ, and the symbol of the Cross, Suzuki wrote earlier:

> Whenever I see a crucified figure of Christ, I can't help thinking of the gap that lies deep between Christianity and Buddhism. This gap is symbolic of the psychological division separating the East from the West. In the East there is no ego. The ego is non-existent and, therefore, there is no ego to be crucified . . . Christ hung helpless, full of sadness on a vertically erected cross. To the Oriental mind, the sight is unbearable![12]

Suzuki's remarks might be true to many Oriental minds, but not necessarily to all. Saint Paul's realization of the Cross of Christ being the power and the wisdom of God is also the experience of several Zen Masters. Zenkei Shibayama wrote:

> It is said that Jesus Christ rose from death after his crucifixion. As I am not a Christian, I do not know the orthodox interpretation of the resurrection in Christianity. I myself believe, however, that Jesus' resurrection means to die in human flesh, and to revive as the Son of God transcending life and flesh. His resurrection means the advent of the kingdom of God. It is the mysterious work of God to create the new and true world. There everybody, everything, lives in God, and all the provisional names and defilements of this earth are never found in the least.[13]

Joshu Sasaki Roshi considered the Crucified Christ as the

One who has reached the state of "unity", or the state of "perfect consciousness", a state in which one is enjoying perfect bliss amidst suffering. He said:

> I consider the Cross to be the symbol of the perfect unity between the suffering and crucifixion of Christ and his enjoyment of perfect bliss. Some of you may think it is strange for me to make the sign of the Cross, but when I make the sign of the Cross, I am embracing the entire universe.[14]

Suzuki has no difficulty accepting Christ as the One saying, "Before Abraham was, I am", or the eternal Christ, but he did not respond to Merton's notion of wisdom along this line. Instead he took up the theme of Innocence which, to him, is identical with Emptiness, or supreme wisdom. This Innocence was found in Paradise. Suzuki wrote:

> The Judeo-Christian idea of Innocence is the moral interpretation of the Buddhist doctrine of Emptiness which is metaphysical, whereas the Judeo-Christian idea of Knowledge epistemologically corresponds to the Buddhist notion of Ignorance. Buddhist philosophy considers discrimination of any kind—moral or metaphysical—the product of Ignorance, which obscures the Original Light of Suchness, which is Emptiness. But this does not mean that the whole world is to be done away with because of its being the outcome of Ignorance. It is the same with Knowledge, for Knowledge is the outcome of our having lost Innocence by eating the forbidden fruit. But no Christian or Jew, as far as I am aware, has ever attempted to get rid of Knowledge in order to regain Paradise, whereby they might enjoy the bliss of Innocence to its full extent as they originally did.[15]

Joseph Chu-Công

Merton's Equation of Emptiness with "Purity of Heart"
Merton liked Suzuki's analysis of Innocence as the supreme wisdom, which prevailed in Paradise before the Fall of man. He wrote:

> As Dr Suzuki makes clear in his analysis of "Innocence", this is really something beyond the level of problem-and-solution. When the monk acts in the primitive emptiness and innocence which the Zen-man calls "suchness" and the Christian calls "purity of heart" or "perfect charity" then the problem does not even arise. As St Paul says, "Against such there is no law".[16]

Suzuki's Emptiness and "Poverty of Spirit"
However, Merton's identification of Suzuki's Emptiness with Christian "purity of heart" did not satisfy Suzuki. In the first place, Suzuki's Emptiness or Suchness is the ultimate wisdom, the supreme truth, whereas Christian "purity of heart", according to the Desert Fathers, is only the immediate end, or a way to the ultimate truth. Secondly, a heart, no matter how pure it is, is a heart, and as long as we still have a heart, we are not fully empty.

Suzuki identifies Emptiness with the Gospel's "poverty of spirit", an attitude of utter dispossessiveness, both exterior and interior. This poverty, according to Suzuki, is the most difficult virtue to practice, more difficult even than meditation.[17] He wrote:

> The subject of poverty is the all-important one in our religious experience—poverty not only in the material but also in the spiritual sense. Asceticism must have as its ground principle a far deeper sense than to be merely curbing human desires and passions; there must be in it something positive and highly religious. "To be poor in spirit", whatever meaning it may have in Christianity, is rich in significance for Buddhists,

especially for Zen followers.[18]

Suzuki is fond of Meister Eckhart's notion of what he calls "die eigenlichste Armut", that is to say, empty of self and of all things. Suzuki wrote:

> We are generally apt to imagine that when the mind or heart is emptied of self and all things, a room is left for God to enter and occupy it. This is a great error. The very thought, even the slightest, of making room for something is a hindrance as monstrous as the mountain.[19]

Suzuki quoted Kyogen Chikan's poem:

> Last year poverty was not yet perfect,
> This year's poverty is absolute.
> In last year's poverty there was room for
>   the head of a gimlet;
> This year's poverty has let the gimlet itself
>   disappear.[20]

Suzuki, then, compared Kyogen Chikan's notion of poverty with that of Meister Eckhart. Eckhart says:

> If it is the case that a man is emptied of things, creatures, himself, and God, and if still God could find a place in him to act, then we say: as long as that place exists, this man is not poor with the most intimate poverty. For God does not intend that man shall have a place reserved for him to work in, since the true poverty of spirit requires that man shall be emptied of God and all his works, so that if God wants to act in the soul, he himself must be the place in which he acts—and that he would like to do. For if God once found a person as poor as this, he would

take the responsibility of his own action and would himself be the scene of action, for God is one who acts within himself. It is here, in this poverty, that man regains the eternal being that once he was, now is, and evermore shall be.[21]

Merton's notion of "purity of heart" is yet not utter emptiness, not utter poverty. It is still the immediate, and not the ultimate end of a monk's life. "Purity of heart" is still in the realm of "created" and not "uncreated" grace. It is still the work of God as the Creator, as Suzuki said, and not God as the Godhead. He wrote:

Father Merton's emptiness, when he uses the term, does not go far enough, I am afraid. I do not know who first made the distinction between the Godhead and God the Creator. This distinction is strikingly illustrative. Father Merton's emptiness is still on the level of God the Creator, and does not go up to the Godhead. So is John Cassian's. The latter has, according to Father Merton, "God's own suchness" as the ultimate end of the monkish life. In my view this way of interpreting suchness is the emptiness of the Creator, not of the Godhead. Zen emptiness is not the emptiness of nothingness, but the emptiness of fullness, in which there is "no gain, no loss, no increase, no decrease," in which this equation takes place:

Zero = infinity.

The Godhead is no other than this equation.[22]

According to Suzuki, Emptiness is Prajna, or transcendental wisdom, and when the description of the working of Prajan is translated into psychological terms, it is a negative phenomenon or an inverse insight, it is a movement towards a position of being unattracted to anything whatever, be it idea or feeling or possession or experience. Thus, Suzuki describes emptiness in this way:

> The Bodhisattva perceives by means of his Prajna-eye the mind of all sentient beings, and he knows how inexhaustibly varied they are in character, in function, response, in moral value, in spirituality, and so on. Yet his perception of "things as they are" penetrates through these superficialities and recognizes that whether their minds are pure or impure, collected or scattered, greedy or not-greedy, they are all devoid of self-substance, of attachment, of discrimination. It is Prajna that sees into all the implications of Emptiness and not the intellect of Vijnana, and they are wise who have opened their Prajna-eye to the truth of Emptiness.[23]

Merton's Hesitation and Suzuki's Dissatisfaction

Merton hesitated to go along with Suzuki on the distinction between God the Creator and the Godhead which, according to him, was condemned by the Church. He subscribed, however, to the theologians of the Oriental Church who distinguished between the "divine energy" through which and in which God "works" outside of himself, and the "divine substance" which is beyond knowledge. This, in fact, was the opinion of many Fathers of the Oriental Church. Casimir Kucharek wrote:

> After Nicea, the Oriental Fathers wisely made the distinction between studying the Divine Being Itself, the Holy Trinity, and the various, exterior manifestations of God, the Trinity known in Its relation to created being. They recognized a distinction between the essence of God, or his nature properly so called, which is unknowable, inaccessible, and his divine energies, or operation, powers proper to and inseparable from God's essence through which he manifests himself, communicates himself, and gives himself.[24]

Suzuki was somewhat disappointed with Merton's many theological divisions and subdivisions. He felt he was not at the same "sapiential and experiential level" with Merton in exchanging his notions on ultimate wisdom. So he wrote:

> I am not acquainted with all the Christian literature produced by the learned, talented, and logically-minded theologians who have endeavored to intellectually clarify their experiences, and therefore, the comments I made on Christianity, its doctrines and traditions, may miss the mark altogether.[25]

Merton also was not too happy with the outcome of the dialogue. As a matter of fact he confessed that his statements on Zen Buddhism were confusing, because he attempted to handle Zen in theological language.[26] There are several points which showed Merton to be a bit confused and unclear in his statements on the life of a Buddhist; for example, he stated:

> For the Buddhist, life is a static and ontological fullness, for the Christian it is dynamic gift, a fullness of love.[27]

It might be true that life in the East, be it in Buddhism or elsewhere still leaves much to be desired as far as its social dynamics is concerned, and thus, Merton's observation can be good food for thought.

The limit of this paper does not allow me to digress on Merton's points of confusion. May it suffice to say that Merton and Suzuki were discussing "Wisdom". But "Wisdom," especially Ultimate Wisdom, either for a Christian or a Buddhist, is anything but static.

The Two Great Friends

At last, however, Merton and Suzuki met personally and they became great friends. Merton was very pleased to hear

Suzuki stressing the importance of "love". He wrote:

> The last words I remember Dr Suzuki saying before
> the usual good-byes were "The important thing is
> love!" I must say that as a Christian I was pro-
> foundly moved. Truly Prajna and Karuna are one
> (as the Buddhists say), or *Caritas* (love) is indeed the
> highest knowledge.[28]

I would like to caution the readers on the notion of "love"
as understood by Suzuki, or by any Zen-man for that matter.
You might be surprised to hear a Zen Master saying that "True
love is the world where there is no love", or "True love does not
belong to the world of language".[29] Suzuki himself would go
slowly, I would think, in accepting Merton's statement that
"Life for a Buddhist is a static, ontological fullness, whereas for
a Christian it is dynamic".

During the joint workshop on Zen Buddhism and Psychoanalysis in Mexico in 1957, conducted by Erich Fromm and
Dr Suzuki and their associates, one of the questions raised to
Suzuki was "How is it that in the writing of Zen there is so little
explicit concern expressed about cultural conditions, the
organization of society and the welfare of man? Do Zen Masters
and students participate in the social problems of today?"
Suzuki answered the question by describing the Zen-man's life,
one aspect of which is "self-sacrificing love". He said:

> Perhaps one of the most noticeable facts in this life
> is that notion of "love" as it is understood by
> Buddhists lacks the demonstrative feature of eroti-
> cism which we observe strongly manifested by some
> of the Christian saints. Their love is directed in a very
> special way toward Christ, whereas Buddhists have
> almost nothing to do with Buddhas but with their
> fellow beings, non-sentient as well as sentient. Their
> love manifests itself in the form of ungrudged and

self-sacrificing labor for others.[30]

In order to illustrate his point, Suzuki, following the Zen Masters' method of teaching, told his audience the following anecdote:

> There was an old woman who kept a teahouse at the foot of Mount Taisan, where there was a Zen monastery known all over China. Whenever a travelling monk asked her which was the way to Mount Taisan, she would say, "Go straight ahead!" When the monk followed her direction, she would remark, "Here is another common churchgoer". Zen monks did not know what to make of her remark. The report reached master Joshu. Joshu said, "Well, I'll go and see what kind of woman she is". He started out and, coming to the teahouse, asked the old lady which road led to Mount Taisan. Sure enough, she told him to go straight ahead, and Joshu did just as many another monk had done. Remarked the woman, "A fine monk, he goes just the same way as the rest". When Joshu came back to the brotherhood, he reported, "Today I have found her out through and through".[31]

Suzuki, then, added his reflection on the incident, saying to his audience:

> We may ask, "What did the old master find in the woman when his behavior was in no way different from that of the rest of the monks?" This is the question each of us has to solve in his own way.[32]

I myself would like to ask "What is Merton's way, what is Suzuki's way?" Or, "What is the Christian way, and what is the Zen Buddhist way?" Mount Taisan was noted for its temple which was supposed to give "wisdom" to the one who worshiped there. The monks asked the woman, who ran the teahouse, the way which led to that Mountain and she answered by saying to them "Go straight ahead!" The woman, presumably an enlightened one, did not mean to tell the monks to take the straight paved road, or way, to the physical mountain, but the straight "Way" that leads to true wisdom, the Way spoken of by both the Zen Masters and Jesus Christ. For example, Lao-Tsu wrote:

> The Way (or Tao) that can be told of
> is not the eternal Way.
> We look at It and do not see It;
> Its name is the Invisible.
> We listen to It and do not hear It;
> Its name is the Inaudible.
> We touch It and do not find It;
> Its name is the Subtle (formless).
> We use It; It is inexhaustible.

The "Way" which the Oriental Sage could neither hear, nor see, nor touch has become visible: the eternal Word of the Father has become Man, Jesus Christ, who spoke of himself:

> I am the Way, the Truth, and the Life.
> No one can come to the Father except through Me.
> I and my Father are one.[33]

This Jesus Christ who is the Wisdom of Merton also seems to be the Wisdom of Suzuki.[34] This Christ is the "Way" where East and West meet. Merton loves the East,[35] and the East loves Merton. Merton came from the West, but Wisdom[36] in her delight brought him to rest on her "other shore"—the Far-East.

Hilary Costello

PILGRIM: FREEDOM BOUND

When Thomas Merton died at the Bangkok meeting in 1968 a lot of people including myself—thought: "Tragic, of course, but how long would he have remained a monk?" To put it in another way, he died just at the right time.

I want to question this judgment. I want to suggest that he died just at the wrong time—just as he was beginning to find the real meaning of his monastic life at its deepest level.

No doubt Merton spent a good deal of time from 1959 till 1965 thinking and writing about non-monastic matters. He was in contact with the "world", he saw the problems of society; he knew many men and women who were involved in the struggle for identity within the totalitarian states of Russia and the capitalistic "slavery" of America. He spoke out in favor of human rights to all men. They were for him years of intense participation. But they brought about a reaction. Evidently he felt he had allowed himself to become too involved, too concerned with the problems of society.

In 1967 Merton was realizing with agonizing conviction that this state of affairs just could not continue. His vocation was to be a monk—in fact, a solitary. And you cannot be a hermit when your hermitage is crowded with visitors. So in 1968 he wrote about his hermitage at Gethsemani: "I still have the feeling that the lack of quiet and the general turbulence there, external and internal, last summer are indications that I ought to move". There were far too many visitors, far too many "worldly" questions that he could not help being involved in and thinking about.

He went to India in the summer of 1968 principally to share the mystical experience of the East, but also partly to reassess his monastic vocation, where he was going, and partly just to get away from Gethsemani for a bit. I am going to leave aside this last motive, because I don't think it is too important. Far more to the point was his continual interest in prayer, contemplation, mysticism. His contacts with the Eastern mystics through his friendship with men like Suzuki and John Wu had created in him a desire to see at first hand what the East had to offer.

Merton was well aware what the Cistercian life was about and what it was not about. It is not a club for untrained farmers; it is not a refuge for amateur intellectuals; still less a genial meeting-place for benevolent liturgists or cheese-makers. You do not come to a monastery merely to study philosophy or to sit in the guesthouse listening to soulful visitors. The whole point of a Cistercian house is that it should leave you free for prayer. But it goes beyond that. Merton saw it as a place where contemplation and mysticism ought to be the ideal; something that monks should be striving after.

Does that mean that we monks are irrelevant to the modern world? To be honest: yes. Merton says: "We live in an ingrained irrelevance which is proper to every human being. The marginal man accepts the basic irrelevance of the human condition, an irrelevance which is manifested above all by the fact of death. He struggles with the fact of death in himself, trying to seek something deeper than death; because there is something deeper than death, and the office of the monk or the marginal person, the meditative person or the poet, is to go beyond death even in this life, to go beyond the dichotomy of life and death and to be, therefore, a witness to life" (*Asian Journal*, p. 306).

It is this struggle to go beyond death to something deeper than death that we must call contemplative wisdom. In the final analysis this is what Cistercian life is all about. Remember Merton's reply to the Dalai Lama about our monastic vows. The Dalai Lama wanted to know whether the vows were some sort of initiation into the mystical life, and whether there was a deep mystical life in our monasteries. Merton's reply was significant: "I said: well, that is what they are supposed to be for, but many monks seem to be interested in something else".

Was Merton himself interested in something else?

During the early 1960s he certainly gives the impression that he was interested in everything else. Almost everyone who came to him in those years would have found him writing and talking about human rights, violence, war, freedom; anything at all except prayer.

But during the last three or four years of his life he was insisting more and more on the "transformation of consciousness" to which monks are called. We would like to know exactly what he meant by this. Is it the same as "Transforming Union"? Is it identical, in other words, with the heights of Christian mysticism as described by St Bernard and St John of the Cross? Merton himself would probably have neither affirmed this nor denied it. Certainly he knew better than anyone else the teaching of St Bernard and St John of the Cross on the subject. He wrote some amazingly insightful articles on it in *Collectanea* during 1948, 1949 and 1950. These articles together with his book *The Ascent to Truth* show that he had a most accurate knowledge of mystical union. He knew what he

69

was talking about. But neither St Bernard nor St John of the Cross would have allowed their descriptions of transforming union outside a totally Christian *milieu*. For them this mystical union was specifically the culminating point of their love of and union with Christ. Transforming union means precisely transformation of love in Jesus. The person who is transformed becomes one with Jesus in love. And quite certainly Merton knew this, for he described it as "a permanent and total transformation in which it becomes literally true to say that the soul has no other life than the life of Christ".

He knew it. He was well aware of the teaching of the great Christian mystics. Yet that last quotation is taken from an article written in 1948. During the subsequent twenty years he had studied Zen Buddhism and other Eastern mystical writings. He was able to compare them at the deep level of common experience, rather than mere intellectual criticism, with the Christian claims. In other words he felt that the Christian West had a lot to learn from the East. Perhaps one of the most explicit statements he made on this point is this: "I need not add that I think we have now reached a stage of (long-overdue) religious maturity at which it may be possible for someone to remain perfectly faithful to a Christian and Western monastic commitment, and yet to learn in depth from, say a Buddhist or Hindu discipline and experience. I believe that some of us need to do this in order to improve the quality of our own monastic life and even to help in the task of monastic renewal which has been undertaken within the Western Church" (*Asian Journal*, p. 131). This is a statement of his own personal ideals, not something that he would have encouraged everyone to aim at. He would have demanded a considerable religious maturity in any person undertaking such a venture, and he would also have insisted on a deep knowledge of both Christian and Eastern mysticism, both by reading and by personal experience of prayer and indeed of contemplation.

He was undoubtedly impressed not only by the mystical teaching of the East but also by the experience of those mystics whom he had personally met and spoken to, and by the similarity between the Christian and Eastern experience. Contemplation is sought by similar disciplines in both. It is seen as a development towards a suprapersonal reality in which a monk endeavors to surmount the limits of the ego and non-ego, the subjective and objective, and to achieve a transcendent mode of perception. Merton was particularly eager for monks of the East and the West to get together and to discuss their mystical ideals in a sort of "mystical ecumenism". This kind of dialogue would be valuable because "both Buddhism and Christianity are alike in making use of ordinary everyday human existence as material for a radical transformation of consciousness" (*A Christian looks at Zen; Thomas Merton on Zen,* p. 109). But he would not have committed himself to saying that the two religions were experiencing the same thing or that mystics "meet at the top", so to speak.

We need to remember that Merton always retained his respect for and real appreciation of western ideals as found in the monastic tradition of his earlier years. This is quite evident when he says: "The monastic and religious culture, handed down from the deeply Christian Middle Ages, has a certain validity of its own. Nor is it totally irrelevant to *all* modern men". No doubt he saw it as a thing of the past—something to which most of us could no longer return—but something which was entirely valid in the 1930s and 1940s. "Many have found", he said, "that Gregorian chant, the reading of the Fathers, monastic ascesis as understood in terms of early Benedictinism and 12th century Cîteaux, the Bible, etc., have helped them find their way to a real self-transcendence, an interior transcendence, an interior transformation, which has met the requirements of their interior call from God". In order to explain what he means by this transformation Merton allows himself a very simple and attractive statement: "Within the structure of monastic life, but not enslaved by externals, they have developed interiorly and acquired a kind of wholeness, certitude and peace" ("Renewal and Discipline", *Cistercian*

Studies, 1970, p. 3).

Nevertheless he turned his face firmly away from this tradition, not because he saw it as irrelevant (which would not have influenced him unduly), but because it had become for him far too confined, because it imprisoned a man in the very restrictive concepts of the past and did not allow him to enter into the heritage of a more universal and more global understanding of truth. Renewal means that the monk, the modern contemplative, must be prepared to share "something of his own solitude and his own awareness of the mystery of Christ with those who come to the Monastery". In practice the monk must be able to listen in depth to and share his experience with those who come from other religious traditions. Merton said explicitly that he was thinking of Buddhists, Hindus, Sufis.

That was why he insisted so much on the need for solitude. For it is only in solitude that a monk of any tradition is able to face himself in all his naked reality. In this solitude, in this self-awareness, in this interior emptiness, "we see that our reality is not a firmly established ego-self already attained that merely has to be perfected, but rather that we are a 'nothing', a 'possibility' in which the gift of creative freedom can realize itself by its response to the free gift of love and peace" ("The Spiritual Father in the Desert Tradition"; *Cistercian Studies,* 1968, p. 3–23).

It needs to be said here, and said with some emphasis, that in 1967 and 1968 Merton was moving further and further away from the involvement in social questions and the themes of violence and peace that had captured his attention in the earlier part of the decade. His output of articles on the subjects dropped dramatically, while his interest in monastic renewal revived. But there was now a marked difference in his approach to monasticism. No longer do we find ourselves in the very restrictive atmosphere of "Trappist" monasticism. By now Merton had extended his vision to include the whole of monasticism, East and West, just as he had immeasurably widened his boundaries of compassion and his understanding of modern social problems. This new freedom of spirit was the fruit of about twelve years of intense struggle. Perhaps this is the reason why an expression like "Transforming Union" is not used by him any more. It is too western, too confined to a particular Christian tradition and to one culture and one spiritual path.

If monastic renewal is to have any real meaning it must be a process of re-education. The monk who has been brought up (as Merton was) in the Catholic tradition of scholastic philosophy needs to imbibe the other great traditions of monastic ideals. "Amor ipse intellectus", quotes Merton, "In plain words, monastic theology has a mystical orientation". So should the philosophy taught in monasteries. It should universalize the monk's understanding of his purpose. "Philosophical training should help the monk to understand those non-Christian traditions of deeply metaphysical contemplation which have flourished especially in Asia". The monk who pursues this line of thought and study might "learn to grasp the characteristic differences between Greek, Hebrew, Indian and Chinese-Japanese modes of thought" ("Renewal in Monastic Education"; *Cistercian Studies,* 1968, p. 259).

One should stress here the need to go far beyond a mere intellectual grasp of these differences. It is only by entering as fully as possible into the heart of these religions that a person will discover their true meaning. Merton was not addressing those who dabble superficially in the odd book or two about comparative religion. He was speaking to those who were willing to seek and pursue the innermost core of belief and love on which the religions were founded. In practice this means praying over a long period of time with the Christian Bible, the Bhagavad Gita, the Upanishad or the Buddhist Sutras as "spiritual reading" and as the subject of contemplation. In this way a person's consciousness will become attuned to the deeper modes of perception that are characteristic of Eastern and Western contemplative traditions. To put it in Merton's own words: "Consequently, Christianity and Buddhism look primarily to a transformation of man's consciousness—a transformation and a liberation of the truth imprisoned in man by ignorance and error" (*Asian Journal,* p. 332-333). Using the traditional Western way of saying the same thing we could speak about "seeking purity of heart" or "resting in the quiet of contemplation".

Now, when Merton discusses this "tranquillity of soul", this "purity of heart", this "quies" (to use the Latin word) that the Desert Fathers sought in order that they might live in the freedom of the sons of God, he is not trying to probe the summit of perfection. In fact, to talk about this summit is to talk nonsense, because it is beyond common-sense and beyond the human perception. "This state of purity and rest", he says, "is not what one can call the 'summit of perfection', whatever that may mean. It is simply the last stage of development that can be observed and discussed in logical terms. It is what John the Solitary calls 'integrity', but his integrity is not the end, it is really the *beginning* of the true spiritual *(pneumatikos)* life. Beyond integrity is mystery which cannot be defined" ("The Spiritual Father in Monastic Tradition"; *Cistercian Studies,* 1968, p. 22).

With all this as his background—and a great deal more, as anyone who has read his books will know—Merton set out in 1968 on his pilgrimage to the Far East. He was primarily seeking for enlightenment; and also seeking for contact with the wise men of the Hindu and Buddhist traditions. But with his strong sense of humor and fun he probably enjoyed the idea of having a rather subtle joke (or "gag") at the expense of some of his critics. He refused to conform to the identity that his earlier works had prescribed for him. He didn't want to remain forever the "pious, rather rigid and narrow-minded monk" that had entered Gethsemani many years before. And he was irritated by the rumor circulating in the U.S.A. that he had left his monastery. "What has actually happened", he protests, "is that I have simply been living where I am and developing in my own way without consulting the public about it since it is none of the public's business" (*Raids on the Unspeakable*). He had no desire or intention of conforming to the blue-print that others had made for him. But he was, all the same, following the daemon that inspired him. He was searching for wisdom: the wisdom of the Far East, the mystical teaching of men like the Dalai Lama, and the Kensho that is sometimes given to the masters of Zen Buddhism. This, yes, he would conform to. So he would give them something to pin their rumors on, and afterwards have a damn good laugh with his friends who really understood what he was getting at.

Merton almost always speaks as a monk: as a monk who is a poet, as a monk who is concerned with many modern problems outside the cloisters; but nevertheless, as a contemplative monk. He continued right to the end in his quest for monastic ideals. For both, East and West "attention must be concentrated on what is really essential to the monastic quest: this, I think, is to be sought in the area of true self-transcendence and enlightenment. It is to be sought in the transformation of consciousness in its ultimate ground, as well as in the highest and most authentic devotional love of the bhakti type—but not in the acquisition of extraordinary powers, in miraculous activities, in a special charismata, visions, levitation, etc. These must be seen as phenomena of a different order" (*Asian Journal*, p. 316. Merton's use of the plural, *charismata*, instead of the singular, *charisma*, must have been a slip of the pen).

He clearly believed that mystical contemplation is not confined to the West or to Christians. On the contrary, it seems that in the East alone do we find a real sympathy for the contemplative ideals which the West has lost. Much of Merton's satire is a pointed reminded that the West has lost its cultural and contemplative roots and has become an empty shell of technology, scientific vanities, urban conglomerations of impersonal persons. Contemplation is indeed supra-personal but grounded in a fully personal experience. It makes a person more human, not less. It is cosmic in its *élan,* and total in its compassion. Merton talks about monastic "work" or mysticism as having a suprapersonal orientation: "It attains to a certain universality and wholeness which have never yet been adequately described— and probably cannot be described—in terms of psychology. Transcending the limits that separate subject from object and self from not-self, this development achieves a wholeness which is described in various ways by the different religions; a self-realization of atman, of Void, of life in Christ, of fana and baga (annihilation and reintegration according to Sufism), etc." (*Asian Journal,* p. 310). I do not claim that Merton is here identifying Transforming Union with the Satori (or Kensho) of Buddhism, but he is not far away from it. He is certainly not confining himself to a Christian experience of God when he says of every discipline that prepares a person for contemplation: "The special formation required to meet the inexpressible conditions (of transformed consciousness) is imparted by experienced persons, or judged by a community that has shared something of the traditional consciousness we may call mystical, contemplative, enlightened or spiritually transformed" (*Asian Journal,* p. 310).

I believe that he was seeking the common ground of contemplative experience in all religions and a common terminology to express it. That was why he felt so strongly the need for dialogue and deep personal exchange between monks of East and West. "We can easily see", he insists with urgent necessity, "the special value of dialogue and exchange among those in the various religions who seek to penetrate the ultimate ground of their beliefs by a transformation of the religious consciousness" (*Asian Journal,* p. 311). He took it as axiomatic that the whole meaning and purpose of monastic life, both East and West, was this special contemplative dedication. Most of us realize only too well that this search is often neglected because of the exigencies of daily life. This is a somewhat dismal fact; not irreversible however. But monks can return to the ideal only if they revive within themselves "a special concern with inner transformation, a deepening of consciousness toward an eventual breakthrough and discovery of a transcendental dimension of life beyond that of the ordinary empirical self and ethical and pious observance" (*Asian Journal*, p. 309).

Naturally Merton was more interested in the monastic quest than in any other subject. It may be true that he concentrated on social questions for a period—under the attraction and the urgency of these problems. But, taken overall, the dominant "thrust" of his life was undoubtedly in the direction of solitude and contemplation. Following on from this we find him discussing the essentials of this monastic quest in terms that echo Zen–Buddhist thought. The purpose of monastic life "is to be sought in the area of true self-transcendence and enlightenment" (*Asian Journal*, p. 316). It is a quest that moves forward towards a deep perception of truth and love. Not just enlightenment; but a loving transformation of the whole person. Indeed it is precisely because contemplation must be unbounded by imagination of particular ideas that it tends to give rise to what may be called a cosmic consciousness. To think of the "Nothing" is to think of the "All". The quiet of contemplation is not the no-thought of boredom or unutterable despair. Quite the contrary, it is the intense gaze that sees beyond things to No-thing, that mounts its resistless flight to the Un-bounded. Insofar as this is possible to all men it may rightly be called a universal consciousness; insofar as it is free from all restrictions it is transcendent. Merton manages to express this with clarity and economy of words: "Above all, it is important that this element of depth and integrity—this element of inner transcendent freedom—be kept intact as we grow toward the full maturity of universal man. We are witnessing the growth of a truly universal consciousness in the modern world. This universal consciousness may be a consciousness of transcendent freedom and vision" (*Asian Journal*, p. 317).

The poet in Merton tended to make him romanticize his experiences. This was particularly true when he found himself in the presence of great natural beauty, such as mountain peaks of looking "down over a waking valley". We find some examples of this in his *Asian Journal.* More especially the tendency becomes suffused with idealism when natural beauty coincides with some perfection of human art. It was only a few days before his death that he "discovered" the statues of Buddhas at Polonnaruwa, about 50 miles North East of Kandy, a town in the mountainous area of central Ceylon (now Sri Lanka). On December 4th he wrote: "I visited Polonnaruwa on Monday. Today is Thursday—which dates the visit to December 1st, nine days before his death. This is important because it was effectively the last major event in his life, and in a certain sense the achievement of all that he was looking for. It left him emotionally speechless. At that moment there was a deep communication or communion between his own ideals and all the mysticism of the East. It spoke to him a message beyond words, too deep and too universal to be defined or even clearly perceived: "I don't know when in my life I have ever had such a sense of beauty and spiritual validity running together in one aesthetic illumination. My Asian pilgrimage had come clear and purified itself. I mean, I know and have seen what I was obscurely looking for" (*Asian Journal,* 231–236).

If there was an element of the romantic about the experience, it was merely incidental; at the deepest level he had an intuition of awe-inspiring unity. It left him speechless because it was immediately apparent to him that Buddhism and Christianity were converging on the same point, striving towards the same or at any rate a similar ultimate transformation. Merton leaves all behind him as he approaches the statues with the utmost sincerity and reverence. They are symbols of a deep cosmic confluence and therefore not to be lightly gazed at: "The vicar general, shying away from 'paganism', hangs back and sits under a tree reading the guidebook. I am able to approach the Buddhas barefoot and undisturbed, my feet in wet grass, wet sand. Then the silence of the extraordinary faces. The great smiles. Huge and yet subtle. Filled with every possibility, questioning nothing, knowing everything, rejecting nothing, the peace not of emotional resignation but of Madhyamika, of sunyata, that has seen through every question without trying to discredit anyone or anything—*without refutation*—without establishing some other argument. For the doctrinaire, the mind that needs well-established positions, such peace, such silence, can be frightening. I was knocked over with a rush of relief and thankfulness at the *obvious* clarity of the figures, the clarity and fluidity of shape and line" (*Asian Journal,* p. 233). Merton is surely saying here that these statues symbolize the state of Nirvana.

His reaction to the Buddhas was a deep feeling of wonder, and later he simply desired to jot down a sort of poetic homage to this wonder. (I feel that the prose of this passage is immensely superior in its poetic feeling to much of the rather artificial and self-conscious "poetry" that he wrote on his pilgrimage). At the time he would have been unable to analyze his feelings or give them a satisfactory philosophical basis. Had he done so he might have had recourse to something like this: "the Buddhist seeks to penetrate the ground of Being and of knowledge, not by reasoning from abstract principles and axioms but by purification and expansion of the moral and religious consciousness until it reaches a state of supra-consciousness or metaconscious realization in which subject and object become one. This realization or enlightenment is called *Nirvana*" (*Nirvana; Thomas Merton on Zen,* p. 129).

Whenever Merton wrote about the correspondence between Zen practice and Christian ideals, he tended to search for harmony by reference to the apophatic tradition of St John of the Cross or Meister Eckhart. *Nirvana* like Christian negative theology is only negative insofar as it endeavors to surpass all that is not All. In its vibrant silence it rises beyond the limitations of human awareness till it becomes one with Pure Being. It is just the opposite of catatonic depression; it is a sort of super-light that is darkness to our intelligence and to the ground of our wonder. External objects are not denied, not even suppressed from consciousness. The mind is not empty like a vacuum; it is only empty to the extent that it is filled with something else, and that something else is No-thing. Merton explains this with his characteristic insight: "The pure consciousness of Zen (as also the apophatic mystical tradition) does not look *at* things, and does not ignore them, annihilate them, negate them. It accepts them fully, in complete oneness with them. It looks 'out of them', as though fulfilling the role of consciousness not for itself only but *for them* also" (*The Zen Koan; Thomas Merton on Zen,* p. 80).

It must be obvious to anyone who has thought about Merton's intense spiritual experience at Polonnaruwa that he saw it as a beginning: an entry into a new mode of monastic life.

His training for the priesthood in scholastic philosophy and Catholic theology had given him a profound knowledge of every strand of Catholic thought. His life in the Cistercian Order had enriched this thought because he had learned by experience over many years the meaning of strict asceticism and a contemplative type of prayer, but also because he had studied closely the great spiritual writers of the Church: Tertullian, Gregory of Nyssa, Augustine, Bernard of Clairvaux, Thomas Aquinas, and especially John of the Cross, and many others. This accounts for his broad knowledge of the Western mystical tradition. Anything that he wrote from about 1948 onwards is deeply affected by these studies and this experience. Indeed it was undoubtedly these factors that earned him his amazing popularity in the first place. He was by choice a journalist and by temperament a poet; and such qualities would have given a sense of immediacy and vividness to his writings, but he was able to add a unique depth to this since he had acquired an immense insight into and knowledge of the great Christian tradition of mystical prayer.

In his earlier writings this was somewhat confined, because by becoming a Cistercian he effectively cut himself off from many aspects of modern thought and modern social problems. Later on, as these problems forced themselves more and more on his attention, he came to realize with growing conviction and compassion that Christ is present in the modern world to the "unbeliever" in a mysterious but powerful way: "The

Lord who speaks of freedom in the ground of our being still continues to speak to every man" (*Conjectures of a Guilty Bystander;* p. 319). One finds him slowly beginning to take a less dismal view not so much of the modern world (of technology and scientific progress) but at least of the men and women who were living out their lives in freedom and love. He steeped himself in the warmer currents of a world-wide sympathy. He began to extend his vision outwards, and to clothe it with the global aspirations of mankind towards the anonymous and hidden Christ. In the light of this new interest he began to write with great respect about the truly contemplative heart of men in all parts of the world, concentrating perhaps a little too much on Japan and India.

Merton was an optimist with a negative slant. His writings often seem to be pervaded with pessimism. But having worked through that pessimism, that rejection of modern technology, that nausea at political maneuvers and the sacred cult of scientific destruction, he suddenly presents us with a devastatingly optimistic intuition: "What is needed is to love all men with a love completely divested of all formally religious presuppositions, simply as our fellow men, men who seek truth and freedom as we do".

A new mode of ecumenism was being initiated. It would aim at uniting all who were seeking the ultimate ground of human understanding and love. During the last ten years of his life Merton had moved steadily forward towards a vision of man on a global scale; he had perceived at a new depth the contemplative aspirations of all men in a way that would have been impossible before the 1950s. His pilgrimage to India and the Far East made it possible for him to confirm at first hand what he was by now convinced of by reading and intuition: namely, that in the final stages of spiritual growth the mystics of all religious traditions, Christians, Hindus, Buddhists or whatever, are somehow united in their communion with "God" and in the transforming effect this has on their consciousness. "Knowing everything, rejecting nothing" means that their love and

81

compassion has been transformed into a total and universal embrace, without limit, without end.

We shall never know what Merton would have done had he returned to Gethsemani Abbey after his pilgrimage. But we can attempt a few conjectures based on our knowledge of his life up to that point. He would no doubt have remained a writer; he would have published his experiences in India and Singapore, and indeed this was done for him posthumously in the *Asian Journal*. He would probably have moved into a more eremitical life than was possible for him at his own monastery. Above all, he was in a unique position to begin a synthesis of Eastern and Western mysticism. Few people had both his knowledge and his ability to fuse into unity all the apparently contradictory elements in the great religious traditions. Perhaps he alone had the sympathy to demonstrate that they are not in opposition but complementary to one another.

But let there be no mistake about it: Merton was a convinced Catholic to the end. There was never any question of him rejecting Catholicism in favor of Buddhism. Right up to his death he desired to remain fully a Christian, fully a Catholic, fully a Cistercian monk. Yet he would certainly have wanted to move deeply into the transcendent freedom that all the great religions propose as an ideal. I am suggesting that by becoming a more perfect Cistercian he would have been even more united with these other traditions. "I am just saying" he insisted in his last talk at Bangkok, "that somewhere behind our monasticism, and behind Buddhist monasticism, is the belief that this kind of freedom and transcendence is somehow attainable".

Lawrence S. Cunningham

HIGH CULTURE
AND SPIRITUALITY

I have always believed that Thomas Merton is intelligible only in terms of his life as a monk.[1] What I wish to discuss here presumes his monasticism but does not often allude directly to it. I wish to present a few reflections on this monk (who was also a reader, a critic, a poet, an artist, and a formidable writer of prose), nurtured in the modernist literary tradition of America as a young man at Columbia University in the thirties who matured into a sophisticated searcher whose intelligence looked both to the South (recall his love for Latin American poets), to the East, and backwards to his own tradition of monastic spirituality and religious mysticism. Most of all I want to reflect a bit on a modern monk who knew our high culture well enough to be in dialogue with it and—perhaps more than he realized—shaped by it.

Encouraged by Woody Allen's *Zelig* I shall let Susan Sontag stand as my spokesman for high culture. In an influential 1967 essay, recently reprinted in *The Susan Sontag Reader,* she begins:

> Every era has to reinvent the project of "spirituality" for itself. (Spirituality—plans, terminologies, ideas of deportment aimed at resolving the painful structural contradictions inherent in the human condition at the completion of human consciousness, at transcendence.)[2]

Sontag's argument for this rather bold beginning is simply put. We live in an age when "art" presents itself as an autonomous reality. We can speak of "art" without meaning a particular art (dance, prose, etc.) or a particular end for art (to decorate, please, instruct, etc.). When art becomes a single genus it simply is as an extension of the artist and, as a consequence, is either an expression of consciousness or—more subtly—an expression of the estrangement of the conscious self. The challenge to the artist is to deal with the *mediacy* of art so that estrangement can be overcome, healed, or abolished. The modern strategy for overcoming the mediacy of art, Sontag insists, is a set of variations designed to overthrow art. These variations are all exercises in forms of silence. The artist can create works of art completely unacceptable to an audience or, like Duchamps, walk away from art, or demand more stringently on silence in art (John Cage), or pare art down to minimal gestures or basic *things* (Samuel Beckett or Jasper Johns).

These various "acts of silence" cannot be taken at face value; they function dialectically so that silence speaks. To pare down, to reduce, to unclutter is, following the paradox, to focus attention and to root out peripheral static from consciousness. What first appears to be modest retirement becomes, in Sontag's words, "an energetic secular blasphemy: the wish to attain the unfettered, unselective total consciousness of God".[3]

The human desire to abolish mediacy for consciousness is not a new one. The ancestors of the modern artists, as Sontag observes, are those who belong to the "radical wing" of the mystical tradition, that tradition in Christianity which begins with the Pseudo-Dionysius and runs through *The Cloud of Unknowing,* Meister Eckhart—the mystical tradition, in short, of the *via negativa.* These mystics bear persistent witness to the desire to leap into direct consciousness just as they bear witness to the need for a subversive language to replace the flabbiness of conventional language of religious experience. The tradition of *via negativa,* Sontag insists, lives, not only in the mystics, but also in the practitioners of non-orthodox psychotherapy and, clearly, in the life of high modernist art.

One cannot read Sontag's essay—or even my partial gloss on it—without thinking of Thomas Merton. Indeed, one so insistently thinks of Merton that for a time I fancied the idea of simply reading chunks of Sontag juxtaposed to snippets from Merton (esp. the Merton of such essays as those in *Raids On the Unspeakable*) and then sit down.

I resisted that approach for two reasons. (1) It in itself is too minimal and arch my purposes. (2) It is overly facile.

From Sontag's essay I do want to underscore one point in particular: the act(s) of silence in the tradition of cultural modernism is rooted in its desire for spareness, lack of adornment, and a concomitant move towards compression—a compression that tightens into enigma and naked gesture. It is the spareness of Kafka and Jasper Johns; it is the silence which haunts the *Four Quartets* and drives John Cage.[4]

The tradition which "pares away" and "grinds down" is one to which Thomas Merton had a great attraction. In thanking Ad Reinhardt—as spare and silent a painter as our culture has produced—for a black on black cross which he desired for his hermitage Merton praised its most noble feature as that of

> its refusal to have anything else around it, notably
> the furniture, etc. It is a most recollected small

> painting. It thinks that only one thing is necessary
> and this is time, but this one thing is by no means
> apparent to one who will not take the trouble to
> look. It is a most religious, devout, and latreutic
> small painting.[5]

The connection between the spare silence of art and contemplation—a common theme in Merton—is most elegantly and compellingly stated in an incident recorded in the posthumously published *The Asian Journal.* It is a moment in Merton's life as epiphanic as his famous "moment" at the "corner of Fourth and Walnut" recorded earlier in his life. At a visit to the great stone buddhas of Ceylon (lovingly photographed by Merton) he, to use his own words, "was knocked over with a rush of relief and thankfulness at the obvious clarity and fluidity of the shape and line, the design and the monumental figures composed into the rock shape and landscape, figure, rock, and tree".[6]
The beauty of these massive stone buddhas provided an insight into the very realities after which Thomas Merton had searched for in his life: the sense of chaste simplicity which is at the heart of reality. On these figures Merton wrote:

> The thing about all this is that there is no puzzle, no
> problem, and really no "mystery". All problems are
> resolved and everything is clear . . . everything is
> compassion. I don't know when in my life I have ever
> had such a sense of beauty and spiritual validity running together in one aesthetic illumination . . . And
> because it needs nothing it can afford to be silent,
> unnoticed, undiscovered.[7]

Note the emphases: "clear"—"empty"—"compassionate" (to be understood in the Buddhist sense)—"needing nothing"—etc. A question naturally arises: how does one reconcile this "paring down" which Merton seeks and relishes with the poetry which he was working on at the time? How reconcile, in short, the chasteness of the Ceylonese buddhas with what seems to be the busily complex surfaces on his long poems "Cables to the Ace" and "The Geography of Lograire"—works he was doing in the late 1960s? One would think that he would have eschewed such heavily laden poetry with the same enthusiasm that his spiritual ancestor St Bernard of Clairvaux bashed the excesses of remanesque sculptual decoration. Or to put it another way: how reconcile the artistic bent of Thomas Merton who practiced endlessly the minimal gesture of calligraphy and the surreal complexities of this late poetry?

A clue may be found in Merton's review essay on the early critical work of Roland Barthes. In a generally favorable assessment of Barthes' critical approach Merton singles out the notion of *gestus* as the "chosen, living, and responsible mode of presence of the writer in the world".[8] True *gestus* occurs only after all the postures have been abandoned and all of the signs of art have been eradicated. The writer is at "zero degree" left only with his writing—the writing is *there* in its nudity. It is that commitment to writing which demands the greatest fidelity; it is writing as the irreducible artifact. Merton then adds:

> What Barthes says about writing corresponds more or less exactly with what Ad Reinhardt said about painting—and said in painting. It is a kind of quietism, if you like; but a deadly Zenlike still out of which—as you find out by reading Barthes himself— there does nevertheless spring a certain inscrutable excitement.[9]

While much of Merton's writing was engaged writing there was a side of him that used writing as another form of calligraphy or as pure *gestus.* Writing could be conceived as marks on paper whose specific structure (and meaning) was to be found, not in the intellectual freight carried by this or that line, but in the very presence of the words in an arrangement. That interest shows up, I think, in Merton's passion for one of the lesser eddies in the poetic stream: concrete poetry. Likewise, the more complex works can be viewed less like a mosaic (a description which Merton proposes for his long poems) and more like a mandala. It would not be otiose, I think, to reread Merton's cullings from Giuseppe Tucci's *The Art of the Mandala* (cited with frequency in *Asian Journal*) while thinking about *Cables to the Ace* and *Geography of Lograire*—this, despite the fact, that the mandala puzzled rather than enlightened Merton.

I have neither the time nor the space to even cursorily discuss these difficult and long late poems but if there is a message in them—or, perhaps, better an "anxiety"—it is the insistent dialectic between Merton's rich and varied reading in the Western and Eastern tradition and his self-distancing from traditional categories of religious thought and monastic categories. There may be truth in Thérèse Lentfoehr's notion that *Cables to the Ace* with its subtitle "Familiar Liturgies of Misunderstanding" may echo Merton's conviction that the public liturgy of the church (remember that this is 1967) "has been rendered inexplicable, incoherent, incommunicable, and no longer capable of being interpreted".[10] As a gestalt *Cables* is intensely self reflective and autobiographical: "I am tormented by poetry and loss". Indeed, I have always thought that the poem, fiercely autobiographical, is set out "there" as the *gestus* of his own sense of self in 1967–68; a poem which was dreamy and surreal; spare and lyrical; complex and simple; erudite and cheeky; cranky and compassionate. It is *there* at a *distance* from the poet as an artifact of his own consciousness.

In that anxious complexity of the late poetry—so seemingly at odds with his drive for simplicity—one finds some compelling links to the high cultural preoccupations of our time. Perhaps more than any other modern Catholic—and certainly more than any other American Catholic—Merton understood the pressures of modern alienation. Despite writing from the depths of a traditional monastery dedicated to a conservative religious vision, he was acutely conscious of those "acids of modernity" (the phrase is Walter Lippman's) which he had first experienced in the Thirties and whose literature he had read all of his life. Part of his monastic vocation—and this I think is obvious to the point of being a truism—was oriented towards a healing therapeutic of the alienation he saw both in his own life and in the life of his times. Merton's interest in the cargo cults and the Amerindian ghost dance (reflected so fully in *The Geography of Lograire*) was not—as he expected it not to be for his readers—purely historical. These religious manifestations are experienced, he wrote, "as yours and mine as well as theirs".[11] Has anyone paid attention to the fact that these religious movements are classic examples of popular reactions, acted out in religious form, to reduce the cognitive dissonance of crumbling cultures eroded, in both cases, through the impact of Western technology and power?

To what degree did Merton see his own Catholic religious vision as a species of cargo cult or his own monastic retreat as a new version of the ghost dance? I do not want to speculate about what Merton's future would have been a decade after his return from Asia. I would say, however, that he was searching for a new vocabulary and a new way of being—perhaps yet in a monastic setting—the newness of which he could not yet clearly articulate. That seems to be implicit both in the biographical data and in the late writings.

Merton came to the Church largely because he discovered a God who rooted and gave significance to all of existence. We all remember the great scene in *The Seven Storey Mountain* when he reads Gilson's *The Spirit of Medieval Philosophy* and sensed in the scholastic concept of God a plenitude to satisfy both his own desire to belong and a sufficient foundation for the world. In his early years he saw God not only as a reality but as Someone who could be reached in a way the power of culture failed to satisfy. It was only the mature Merton, in a famous retraction, who was able to reconcile his poetry and contemplative life into a single whole.[12]

At the end of his life Merton, I feel, was able to reaffirm

that deep center and foundation once again but it was no longer in the vocabulary of the schoolmen. What happened before the Buddhas in Ceylon could not be formulated in the language of metaphysics. It was—as the mystics always knew— that the language of metaphysics falters in the ultimate ascent. Perhaps that is why, when *Cables to the Ace* was finally finished, he went back and made some prose additions to the poem; cullings from the Zen Masters and the Rhineland mystics. It was to that language—oxymoronic, spare, poetic,— that his vision led him for it is a language whose silence, as Sontag says, is "loud" as it tries to hold in balance the unstable antithesis between plenum and void.[13]

Merton worked out his strategy in the context of Christian monasticism but his imagination was catholic in the more general sense of the word. It engaged, shaped, and distanced itself from the flotsam of his omnivorous reading and his deep hunger for silence and reconciliation. That death should have cut him off is a great tragedy for American Catholicism. His taste for Eastern wisdom combined with his deep feeling for our history in all of its textured modernism was leading him to a spirit of compassionate silence which even today, incomplete as it is, speaks loudly and clearly of our deepest perplexities and their possible remedies.

Patrick Hart

A MONASTIC
EXCHANGE
OF LETTERS:
LECLERCQ
and MERTON

My first reaction to reading the correspondence between Fathers Jean Leclercq and Thomas Merton was one of amazement. When the exchange of letters began between these two monks separated by the Atlantic Ocean, Thomas Merton was a Cistercian monk recently ordained to the priesthood (1949), becoming more and more involved with the monastic formation of the young monks at the Abbey of Gethsemani. Meanwhile, Jean Leclercq in his monastery of Clervaux in Luxembourg, was deeply engrossed in his work on the critical edition of the works of St. Bernard of Clairvaux, and was already publishing studies on medieval writers. So naturally the first letters dealt mainly with monastic subjects, but this later broadened to include renewal, social justice and the place of the monk in an increasingly troubled world.

The first exchange concerned making films of some text of St Bernard that was among the rare books of the Obrecht Collection at Gethsemani. These manuscripts and incunabula were eventually transferred to the Institute of Cistercian Studies at Western Michigan University in Kalamazoo, where they are made available to scholarship. But the very first extant letter of the correspondence implies at least one missing letter. Merton writes of another film of the St Bernard Sermons now on its way. Apparently the first attempt proved less than successful. And Merton uses the occasion to invite Leclercq to come to Gethsemani. I will quote directly from this letter, which opened the correspondence, as well as subsequent letters, which manifest a monastic collaboration of unusual significance:

"I might wish that your travels would bring you to this side of the Atlantic and that we might have the pleasure of receiving you at Gethsemani. We have just remodeled the vault where our rare books are kept and have extended its capacities to include a good little library on Scripture and the Fathers and the Liturgy—or at least the nucleus of one. Here I hope to form a group of competent students not merely of history or of texts but rather—in line with the tradition which you so admirably represent—men competent in all-round spiritual theology, as well as scholarship, using their time and talents to develop the seed of the word of God in their souls, not to choke it under an overgrowth of useless research as is the tradition in the universities of this country at the moment . . . Our studies and writing should by their very nature contribute to our contemplation, at least remotely, and contemplation in turn should be able to find expression in channels laid open for it and deepened by familiarity with the Fathers of the Church. This is an age that calls for St Augustines and Leos, Gregorys and

Cyrils!" [Letter of Merton to Leclercq, 22 April 1950].

Merton continues in the next paragraph to compliment Leclercq on his own contribution in this area. "That is why I feel that your works are so tremendously helpful, dear Father. Your *St Bernard Mystique* is altogether admirable because, while being simple and fluent, it communicates to the reader a real appreciation of St Bernard's spirituality. You are wrong to consider your treatment of St Bernard superficial. It is indeed addressed to the general reader but for all that it is profound and all embracing and far more valuable than the rather technical study which I undertook for the *Collectanea* [these studies were later published under the title *Merton on St Bernard*, Cistercian Publications, 1980, with an introduction by Jean Leclercq] and which, as you will see on reading it, was beyond my capacities as a theologian".

In a letter dated May 5, 1950, Father Jean responded to Merton with the following words [which display how lightly he wore his scholarship:] "Thank you also for your prayers and encouragement. I know that some scholars and professors criticize my books because they are too 'human', not sufficiently or purely 'scientific', objective: but I do not care about having a good reputation as a scholar among scholars, although I could also do pure scholarly work, and I sometimes do, just to show that I know what it is. But I also know that many monks, and they are the most monastic monks, in several Orders—Camaldolese, Cistercians, Trappists, Benedictines of the strictest observances—find my books nourishing, and find in them an answer to their own aspirations. I thank God for that, my only merit—if any—is to accept not to be a pure scholar; otherwise I never invent ideas: I just bring to light ideas and experiences which are to be found in old monastic books that nobody, even in monasteries, ever reads today" [Letter of Leclercq to Merton, 5 May 1950, translated by Sr Bernard Said, O.S.B.].

Father Jean, in this same letter, then writes of Father Louis' own question of finding the proper balance between work and prayer and contemplative leisure: "I think you have an important job to do at Gethsemani: first for America, and then for the whole Cistercian Order: to come back to the Cistercian ideal. But there are two difficulties. The first is to keep the just measure in work, either manual or intellectual. Both forms of work, and especially the second, entail a danger of activism (mental activism), multiplicity and complexity, which are contrary to monastic 'simplicity': that is a personal question which each monk has to solve for himself if he wants to work and stay a monk; some are unable to do both and have to choose to remain monks. The second difficulty is more of the historical order, if we want to study the Cistercian tradition. I am alluding to the illusion of believing that the Cistercian tradition began with Cîteaux. I am becoming more and more convinced that the Cistercian tradition cannot be understood without its roots which were in pre-existing and contemporary Benedictine—and generally, monastic—tradition. That is why in my studies I never separate the different forms and expressions of the unique monastic thought and experience. For instance, if one begins to study the Mariology of the Cistercian school without taking into consideration previous and contemporary monastic thought at the time about the Virgin, then one tends to think that the Cistercians were at the origin of all true and fervent Mariology. Yet if one recalls what St Anselm and the monks of the Anglo-Norman eleventh century wrote, then possibly one might come to the conclusion that in this field Cistercians, far from making progress may even have retrograded (I think, for example, of the Conception of Our Lady). The only way to avoid such pitfalls is to be quite free from any order-emphasis, any 'order politics', and to search solely for the truth in the life of the Church of God".

Later in the same letter, Father Jean responds to Merton's own writings by saying that he had received *The Waters of Siloe* and had just completed the Prologue: "So far, I must say that I thoroughly enjoy your pages: both what you say and the way you say it. I think that one immediately feels that you 'believe' in the contemplative life, and this faith of yours is more forceful for convincing your readers than would be the most scientific treatment of the subject. In my opinion, you point out the very essence of monastic life when you say that it is a contemplative life. The Benedictine tradition is certainly a contemplative tradition: the doctrine of Benedictine medieval writers (and almost always up to our own days—the twentieth century is an exception, alas!) is a doctrine of contemplation and contemplative life. But we must confess that Benedictine history is not entirely—and in certain periods not at all—contemplative. Nevertheless, even when Benedictines were busy about many things, they never made this business *circa plurima* an ideal, and they never spoke about it; their doctrine was always that of the *unum necessarium*".

On July 29, 1950, Jean Leclercq writes to Merton thanking him for his "long and interesting letter of June 17" which unfortunately has been lost. Father Jean speaks of Merton's approval of an article on *lectio divina* in the following lines: "I am glad you approve what I wrote about *lectio divina*. I do not think that we must try to settle an opposition between the spiritual and the scientific reading of the Scriptures: we must try to reconcile these two methods as was the case in the middle ages, when the same doctors explained the Bible using both methods. I tried to explain this in a paper to be published in the collection (ed. du Cerf) about *L'exégèse de l'Ancien Testament:* 1) In the middle ages there were two sorts of exegetics: scientific and spiritual; 2) but there were not two sorts of scripture scholars: all used the two methods; 3) and these two methods of scripture study supposed the same conception of Holy Scripture, and especially the relations between the Old and the New Testament".

Father Jean then goes on in this same letter to write of what he thinks the monk's task today is in this area: "I think that the way of teaching the Bible now common in our theological colleges is merely apologetic, which was probably very useful forty years ago. Now, thanks to a reaction against this apologetic reaction, we are finding the *via media,* the *via conciliatonis non oppositionis.* One of the tasks of the monastic world today is to give a practical demonstration that this reconciliation is possible: we should not reject the results of modern biblical sciences, but neither should we be satisfied with them".

Father Jean continues on the subject of oriental mysticism and St Bernard: "I am not sufficiently acquainted with oriental mysticism to have an opinion on yoga and St Bernard. But since all mystical experiences are fundamentally the same, there is surely some connection; and this not only in the experience itself; but also in the expression of it. From this point of view I think that depth pyschology will shed some light on these profound and universal themes of the religious representation".

And finally, in this same extraordinary letter, Leclercq writes of Merton's desire for the solitary life, which implies that the now lost letter dealt with this subject. "I quite understand your aspirations to a solitary life. I think there has always been an eremitical tradition in the Cistercian and the Benedictine Orders. In my opinion we are not to discuss personal vocation according to principles of community life, nor according to universal laws. We must always be very respectful of these vocations, provided they are real vocations and not illusions. Personally, though I am quite inept for the eremitical life, I have always encouraged my confreres who aspire to such a life. Now, in France, there are some Benedictine monks who live as hermits in the mountains. Nobody knows it except God. The tradition of hermitages near monasteries or *'inclusi'* in monasteries seems very difficult to revive today. So we must find some new solutions to this problem. It is a permanent problem and one which is a very good sign of the monastic fervour of the times: whenever cenobia are what they ought to be, they produce inevitably some eremitical vocations. The eremitic vocations disappear in times and countries where monasticism has ceased to be monastic".

From the above quotation, one can see that the correspondence shifts from abstract considerations of the renewal of the *ordo monasticus* to more personal existential questions. In short, Merton had such confidence and trust in Leclercq's judgment that he was seeking counsel and advice as his own solitary vocation matured. Merton responds in his October 9, 1950, letter, which begins: "It is a long time since I received your July letter which I read and pondered with deep satisfaction. It is a privilege for which I am deeply grateful, to be able to seek nourishment and inspiration directly from those who keep themselves so close to the sources of monastic spirituality".

Merton then picks up on their previous exchange on St Bernard and his meditation on the Scriptures: "Your remarks on St Bernard's ideas of Scripture are extremely important to me. I have been meditating on your appendix to *Saint Bernard Mystique,* and also I have been talking on this very subject to the students here. I agree with your conclusions about Saint Bernard and yet I wonder if it would not be possible to say that he did consider himself in a very definite sense an exegete. My own subjective feeling is that the full seriousness of St Bernard's attitude to Scripture is not brought out entirely unless we can in some sense treat him as an exegete and as theologian, in his exposition of the Cancticle. Naturally he is not either of these things in a purely modern sense. But I think he is acting as a theologian according to the Greek Fathers' conception, at least to some extent . . . I think that is essentially what you were saying when you brought out the fact that he was seeking less to nourish his interior life than to exercise it. As if new meanings in his own life and in Scripture spontaneously grew up to confirm each other as soon as Bernard immersed himself in the Sacred Text. Still, there is the evident desire of the saint to *penetrate* the Text with a certain mystical understanding and this means to arrive at a living contact with the Word hidden in the word. This would be tantamount to saying that for Bernard, both exegesis and theology found their fuller expression in a concrete mystical experience of God in His revelation".

After thanking Father Jean for his words on the vocation

to solitude, Merton closes this letter as follows: "Once again, dear Father, thank you for your advice and inspiration. May Jesus bless your great work for His glory and for the vitality of monasticism everywhere. Pray for me in my turn to be more and more a child of St Benedict—and if it be God's will, that I may some day find a way to be something of an eremitical son of St Benedict, yet always in the cadre of Cîteaux. An interesting problem? What of these Benedictines in the mountains of France? Have you more information about them? I am not inquiring in a spirit of restlessness! Their project is something I admire on its own merits".

Leclercq responds to this letter from Paris on the 26th of October picking up the theme of St Bernard as theologian: "Of course, I agree that St Bernard was a theologian in the traditional sense of the word: *loqui Deo de Deo.* This meaning has been preserved in the monastic tradition, and I explained that in my *Jean de Fecamp.* I am coming to notice more and more how much not only St Bernard, but the whole monastic world of the twelfth century, Cistercian and Benedictine, is full of Origen. I gave a lecture on this subject three weeks ago at Chevetogne, and I have been asked to publish it in *Irenikon.* In it I pointed out this relation between the Greek Fathers and medieval monasticism. I had already dealt with the question in a very general way in 1945. Now I see things better. Maybe I shall collect everything I find on the matter and write a little article. The works of Origen which have been the most read by monks are his commentaries on Holy Scripture. And it is his exegesis, more than his doctrine, which influenced monks and Bernard".

Father Jean discusses several other ideas that Merton put forward in his last letter, but then comes to the question of solitude again, which was very close to Merton's heart: "About the eremitical vocation: it is clear that the Cistercian vocation and life are, in themselves, eremitical. So a Cistercian, normally, should not have to seek this anywhere else than in his enclosure. The Cistercian's solitude depends on his silence. But it may happen that for accidental and psychological reasons, for example, if there are too many monks in the same monastery, or if a monk has too much to do, he longs for more silence. Then I think that the solution for him is to change his monastery and seek for silence and quiet elsewhere, in another Cistercian monastery".

This last statement is interesting, since Leclercq's advice is so balanced and nuanced, and shows great discretion when he suggests a transfer only when the local situation becomes impossible and then only to "another Cistercian monastery". It is obvious from this that Father Jean was in no way trying to disturb community life, but simply responding to a pastoral need with very wise counsel.

From 1950 there seems to have been little correspondence until 1953. Merton had sent Leclercq a copy of *The Sign of Jonas* when it came out in the early part of the year. In his letter of March 17th, 1953, Father Jean thanks him for the book, and for the first time writes in English. "As you are accustomed to receiving praise, I shall not send you one more letter of that sort. I'll just say that I surveyed your book and I liked it. I think that I shall read it when I find time. It is written with this kind of freshness, a little 'primitive' that we like in Americans (I suppose you accept me speaking to you simply, like a monk to a monk). I think this book with *Seeds of Contemplation* is exactly the kind of book you are made to write". He then goes on to suggest the idea of publishing *The Sign of Jonas* journal in French in a series called *Tradition monastique,* of which Father Leclercq was one of the directors.

Leclercq then mentions some criticism that appeared in Europe upon the publication of *The Ascent to Truth,* a book of Merton's dealing with the theology of St John of the Cross and the Spanish mystics. But then Father Jean softens it by saying: "But these are the sort of criticisms that Europeans are prepared to make. And the Church is everywhere, in the Old and the New World. In Europe we are so complicated: textual criticism has come to have such importance. We cannot even quote the *Pater noster* without putting a reference in the footnotes".

About this time, Leclercq had published a book on the doctrine of Blessed Paul Giustiniani, which concerned the eremitical life of the Camaldolese. This prompted an enthusiastic response from Father Louis in which he writes: "Above all I want to thank you for your *Doctrina del B. P. Giustiniani* [this volume was later translated into English and published by Farrar, Strauss, with an introduction by Thomas Merton]. I find it most useful and am glad to have it, particularly because it would otherwise be quite impossible for me to make the acquaintance of his personality and ideas. You have given us a valuable source". After commenting on the beauty of the Camaldolese ideal and "the true contemplative life of Frascati", he asks Father Jean for photographs of that particular eremo, since he was considering writing an article on the Camaldolese and wanted to help them in preparing for a foundation in the United States. He ends his letter with another request for prayers: "Thank you for your prayers: I need them. And I hope they will obtain for me more and more solitude and obscurity and the humility proper to a true monk" [Merton to Leclercq, 21 August 1953].

In a letter of November 5, 1953, Father Louis writes Father Jean of his satisfaction in receiving permission from the Abbot to write an introduction to the Leclercq volume on Paul Giustiniani, and comments: "I feel that it is especially important that the true place of the solitary in the Church should be brought out at this time when there are so many who despise contemplation and when even in the monastic orders there is a tendency to go off the right road precisely because the values for which the solitary exists are not appreciated". He continues how pleased he was that the Abbot of Gethsemani had invited Father Leclercq to give the community retreat although the latter expressed his difficulties with the English language. Father Louis encouraged him to come in any case, and concludes: "I certainly agree wholeheartedly that the monastic orders have much to learn from one another, and we in America have much to learn from you in Europe. We are very isolated and provincial, I am afraid, and our undue sense of our own importance may perhaps delude us that we are the only monks in the world. It may not be possible to me to satisfy the desires of my own heart, but at least I can continue to have zeal for God's truth and for the monastic ideal".

During 1954 there is a considerable exchange of letters in reference to the publication of Merton's book on Bernard of Clairvaux and his commentary on the encyclical of Pope Pius XII on the mellifluous doctor, *The Last of the Fathers*. Dealing with foreign agents and translators was something of a burden for Merton, and he tended to turn it over to others. Since he was rather impractical in publishing affairs, there often resulted tangles with publishers and translators and agents, including, of course, the censors of the Order, who had to approve not only the original manuscripts, but each translation. In France, in particular, this caused him a great deal of pain.

In making reference to the difficulties he was having with censors of *The Sign of Jonas* he continued in a letter of July 28, 1954: "It is true that religious in Europe are not yet used to journals, but the secular reader in France certainly has begun to acquire a taste for them. Witness the success of the Journals of Gide, Green and Du Bos. I am glad my own Journal [*Sign of Jonas*] will be expurgated, but in the long run it would seem to be not a bad idea that, for once, by way of exception, such a production should come from a monastery. I would give anything for a journal, even the most trivial, written in 12th century Clairvaux. But then, indeed, they did *not* keep journals".

Although the Abbot General, with the advice of the various censors, decided against the publication of this journal, thanks to an impassioned plea from Jacques Maritain to the French General, the decision was reversed and the book was allowed to be published—not only in English, but in many other languages.

Some years later, another journal, *Conjectures of a Guilty Bystander,* as well as the posthumous *Asian Journal* were published from his private journals.

It was clear from his letter of July 28, 1954, to Leclercq that Merton enjoyed this kind of monastic collaboration and he makes a promise of even further cooperation on a book of meditations that eventually was published in this same series: (*Thoughts in Solitude,* 1957—This volume was published in France under the title *Les chemins de la joie*) "Please tell your good Father Abbot that I feel that I am really doing the work of God in collaborating as much as I can with your series, and will feel that my own writing is thereby inserted in a truly monastic context. There is a special satisfaction in collaborating with one's brothers in Christ, and I do not like the idea of an isolated, and spectacular, apostolate. No doubt I must have the courage to face the enemies that this isolation makes for me—even among priests and religious. But for my own part I prefer to be a member of a team, at least to some extent, than to be a soloist exclusively. However, since God has singled me out for a kind of isolation I will certainly accept it, together with its consequences. This is certainly nothing new in the Church".

During the next several years there was considerable correspondence, some of which exists, but many other letters were lost, which deal with Merton's desire for greater solitude, even to the extent of a possible transfer to the Camaldolese or Carthusians. Neither plan materialized. Father Leclercq during this time of crisis was kept aware of the situation and offered advice and counsel as best he could from such a distance. Father Louis was made novice master in the summer of 1955 and soon after wrote to Father Jean: "As time goes on it seems that I grow closer to the state in which nothing at all is written. I have not attempted anything like a book since I became novice master . . . The question of solitude is no longer any kind of question. I leave everything in the hands of God and find my solitude in His will, without being theatrical or glowingly pious about it. I am content. But the right kind of contentment is a perfect solitude. When one is more or less content with 'nothing' that is at hand, one finds in it everything. I do not mean 'nothing' in a tragic, austere sense, but the plain nothing which is the something of every day. The life of a Benedictine does not require all the fierce strippings of a St John of the Cross, but the common way without exaltation (even in nothingness) is enough" [Undated fragment of a letter of Merton to Leclercq which can be traced to the Fall of 1956].

On May 22, 1959, Father Louis wrote to Father Jean after a considerable silence: "Most of the trouble comes from the fact that I have been out of contact with you for so long. It is a pleasure to greet you again, and to ask your prayers. I hear Dom Jacques Winandy is in Martinique. I hope he will pray for me too. I naturally keep a certain desire for solitude in my heart and cannot help but hope that some day it may be realized. But I no longer have any thought or desire of transferring to another Order. I believe that to move from one institution to another is simply futile. I do not believe that there is any institutional solution for me. I can hope however that perhaps I might gain permission to live alone, in the shadow of this monastery, if my Superiors will ever permit it. I do not think that there is any other fully satisfactory way for me to face this, and to seek to live my own life with God. I am not pushing this, however, simply praying, hoping and waiting".

In a letter dated December 31, 1960, Father Jean responds: "I am glad to know that your personal problems are solved. I think you (they) finally came across the traditional solution, for those who need it and it ought to be found within the institution itself. You call for a western Athos: but that was traditionally realized in medieval monasteries, when the institutions were flexible enough to give different sorts of souls different ways of living the same monastic life".

But that was not the end of Merton's eremitical yearnings, nor of his writing on the subject. After several years of comparative quiet, Merton writes to Leclercq on June 10, 1963: "Things are developing well here . . . I received permission to take some time in solitude up at the hermitage, and so far I have had six full days up there, with more to come. Not allowed to sleep there, or say Mass there, but what I have had so far is a great godsend. It has certainly settled any doubts I may have had about the need for real solitude in my own life. Though I realize that I am not the ideal of any absolute hermit, since my solitude is partly that of an intellectual and poet; still it is a very real inclination for solitude and when I have continuous solitude for a more or less extended period, it means a great deal and is certainly the best remedy for the tensions and pressures that I generate when I am with the community. It is indeed the only really satisfactory remedy that I have been able to find. Distractions and 'recreations' with visitors and active retreat work, etc. do absolutely nothing to help. Also this little bit of solitude helps me to appreciate the real values that do exist in the common life, though they certainly manage to get hidden when I get too much of them. I hope to take more time in retreat later in the summer or in the early fall. And perhaps get a day at a time, more frequently".

Merton's hermitage, which was constructed in 1960, was originally intended as a place for ecumenical dialogue with professors and students from local Baptist, Disciples of Christ or Episcopalian seminaries. Later, as the above quoted letter indicates, he was able to spend more time in solitude at this quiet retreat on Gethsemani's property. On August 20th, 1965, the Feast of St Bernard, Merton was finally given permission to give up his post as novice master and enter into the solitary life of a hermit full time. Well, not exactly, since he was still expected to return to the monastery for the main meal each day, and offer Mass in the Library Chapel. He also served on the Abbot's Council and gave a weekly conference to the monks. (Only in the spring of 1968 was the chapel finally completed as an addition to the hermitage so he could offer Mass each day there.) This was a direct result of the General Chapter's approval of hermits within the Order at the 1965 Chapter. Merton writes of it to Leclercq: "Yes, I was a bit surprised that the General Chapter even officially and publicly admitted that a Cistercian could become a hermit without the Order collapsing. It seems definite that I will be able to do this, and I am in fact spending most of my time in the hermitage . . . " [Letter of Merton to Leclercq, dated July 5, 1965].

Merton's first letter to Leclercq after entering upon the hermit life was dated September 18, 1965, and expresses his delight: "For the first time in twenty-five years I feel that I am leading a really 'monastic' life. All that I had hoped to find in solitude is really here, and more. At the same time I can see that one cannot trifle with solitude as one can with the common life. It requires great energy and attention, but of course without constant grace it would be useless to expect these. Hence I would very much appreciate your prayers. But in any case it is good to have this silence and peace, and to be able to get down to the *unum necessarium*". In the same letter it is rather ironic to read of his disappointment at not being given permission to attend a meeting of theologians and scholars at St John's Abbey, Collegeville: "It is a great pity I was not able to be at Collegeville. Some people think there is a conflict between solitude and rare, exceptional meetings of this kind. I do not. I think they go together, and I am not of the opinion that the hermit is supposed to be so superior to all others that he cannot profit by humbly listening to what they have to say and learning from them . . . . But the principle does remain, and if God wills solitude for me I take it entirely on His terms. If He wants it to be absolute, that is fine. I am glad at any rate that you thought of saying a word on my behalf. I feel very ashamed for not having been able to come, especially because of this implication of 'superiority' which is so silly".

Responding to a letter of Leclercq from Africa where he reported on the new monastic developments there, Merton writes: "Thanks for your good card from Africa. I have sent some mimeographs and books to the monks of Hanga, and

I hope they will be able to get something out of them. I am always delighted to be of use if I can, and thus justify my miserable existence. Actually, it is not miserable at all and I am getting more and more roots in solitude so that the hermitage is to me the only conceivable kind of life. I do not claim that I am an ideal hermit, but then neither was I an ideal cenobite. I will probably cause less scandal being hidden in the woods; hence everything points to the fact that I am where I belong. But it is really an excellent life. Time takes on a completely different quality and one really lives, even though nothing apparently happens at all. The direction is all vertical, and that is what matters, though at the same time one is not conscious of it".

In accepting an invitation to visit Gethsemani, Father Jean writes to Merton in a letter of August 16, 1966, about giving conferences to the community and then adds: "I am more and more interested in attempting to integrate the new trends in Christology, Biblical studies, psychology, meta-physics with reflection and interpretation of monastic spirituality. It is not easy, but gratifying even so. I had a glorious time with Father du Lubac a few days ago when we talked about all that (Did you know that he encouraged your confrere [a monk of Gethsemani did a doctoral dissertation at Sant'Anselmo in Rome on Teilhard and St Bernard] working on Teilhard and St Bernard?) I have also made some recent discoveries about St Bernard. No new texts; but new insights. I shall greatly profit by a discussion with you about this".

Back in Rome, Father Leclercq had come to Merton's defense at Sant'Anselmo to which Father Louis writes in appreciation on November 18, 1966: "Thanks for having the courage to defend someone that most people apparently don't know what to make of. That is an element of my solitude, but I do not grudge you bringing me this kind of welcome company. The desert is never absolute, or should not be! Seriously, it is a consolation to find oneself after all part of the Catholic Church and not excommunicated without appeal . . . Many thanks for your charity and, I think, your objectivity too. It helps me to evaluate my own life and my own position in the Church". He continues in the same letter saying he is sending a copy of *Conjectures of a Guilty Bystander,* another journal, although not spiritual, which many will find disconcerting; he suggests an alternative title: *The Subjunctives of a Guilty Bartender!*

Father Leclercq had sent Merton a collection of letters of the former's Asian journey, which Father Louis found fascinating and suggested bringing it out in book form. Merton comments: "It was comforting to note that all the places where you found some reality and life of prayer were places that had at least some remote connection with Cîteaux (as for example the foundations of La Pierre qui Vire) and I am glad the Trappists of Indonesia were good. Of Kurisumali I had long had a very good impression, but I was happy to learn of the others. As to the corruption that American civilization is bringing with it—that is a source of more and more sorrow to me".

Little did he know that a year from this time he would be making plans for his own journey to the East, and India in particular. And it was Father Jean Leclercq who was most instrumental in arranging for the invitation to come. But in November of 1967 he was again writing to Father Jean telling him of the news of Dom James' retirement as Abbot and of an abbatial election in which the new Abbot may be more open to his accepting invitations to travel and give retreats and talks. He reflects on his own situation as follows: "I get innumerable invitations which I have to refuse, and my decision is that since I am a hermit I shall continue to do so. That is to say that I will not appear anywhere in public or semi-public, anyhow. Do you agree that this is a good decision for me? I think it is best that I stay out of the mainstream of things and mind my own business. It is true, I will fail to learn things and be less well informed, but I think it is my lot to engage in something else and do my own work, quite apart from what others may be doing" [Merton to Leclercq, November 10, 1967].

A jubilant letter of January 14, 1968, from Father Louis

announces a new Abbot of Gethsemani in the pontifical manner: "Annuntio tibi gaudium magnum: habemus abbatem—I waited for the election before replying to your letter. Fr Flavian is our new Abbot. Certainly the best man we have for the job at the moment, and I think that eventually he will consent to my going. I am most anxious to attend the meeting and believe it will be fruitful. Certainly I am convinced that it is very important for me to meet some Eastern monks and also see some of our own Christian monasteries out there".

By return mail, Father Leclercq sent the formal invitation to attend the Bangkok meeting, which Father Louis presented to Abbot Flavian. The latter was at first hesitant as Merton writes in his January 30th letter to Leclercq: "Many thanks for your letter of the 21st about the Bangkok meeting. I have discussed it with the new Abbot, Dom Flavian. As yet the discussion has been inconclusive. Dom Flavian is quite open to the proposal, but does not believe that he has the authority to simply grant me permission for the journey". He goes on to suggest various people who might write to the Abbot to encourage him, such as Archbishop McDonough of Louisville, Abbot de Floris, the Director of the A.I.M., as well as Cardinal Vagnozzi. He concludes this letter with hopes for future journeys as well: "I do hope that I can participate in it with you, and would love to travel out there with you via Japan. Also, of course, I would very much like to be at the African meeting. It is necessary that I finally learn something about what is going on and attendance at these meetings is one essential way of getting some reliable information".

Although some of these letters of the spring and summer of 1968 are missing, or perhaps carbons were not made, the final permission of Abbot Flavian for the proposed Asian journey came in the spring of 1968, sometime after March 8th. In a letter of that date to Leclercq, Merton mentions that the Abbot was seriously considering the matter, but had not come out with a definite yes or a definite no. By July, however, the decision was made in favor of the trip, and Father Louis writes to Father Jean: "Thanks for your good letter about the arrangements for Bangkok. I will be glad to give the talk on Marxism and so on. [Marxism and Monastic Perspectives] Important indeed! I've familiarized myself pretty well with Herbert Marcuse whose ideas are so influential in the 'student revolts' of the time. I must admit that I find him closer to monasticism than many theologians. Those who question the structures of contemporary society at least look to monks for a certain distance and critical perspective. Which alas is seldom found. The vocation of the monk in the modern world, especially Marxist, is not survival but prophecy. We are all busy saving our skins" [Merton to Leclercq, July 23, 1968].

These monastic friends of two decades met once again in Bangkok, a couple of days before the meeting of monastic leaders of the Far East. Father Louis wrote me on December 8th, having arrived two days before in Bangkok, saying how happy he was to see Father Jean again, who was his enthusiastic and lively self. By the time Father Louis' letter reached Gethsemani, news of his death had already arrived. It has seemed singularly appropriate that these two monks who were so deeply involved in the renewal of the *ordo monasticus* should have their final meeting amidst monks and nuns of Asia whose presence has symbolized the most authentic contemplative spirit, the very heart of the monastic vocation as seen and loved by both Jean Leclercq and Thomas Merton.

Victor A. Kramer

POETRY
AS EXEMPLIFICATION
OF THE
MONASTIC JOURNEY

Father Louis, as he was known in religious life, was a prolific author perhaps best known for his autobiographical writing and essays on topics which ranged from questions about the solitary life to the relationship of the contemplative vocation to the modern world. As a spiritual commentator and conscience for others, his calling as a writer was often to raise questions for those who lived beyond the monastery; however his best writing almost always reflected his monastic way of life too. In this essay I will raise questions about Merton's poetry as a reflection of the interior journey a monk makes within the setting of a contemporary Cistercian atmosphere; it is signifi-cant that this is a journey made always in relation to an awareness of the larger community. One of the significant things about Merton's poetry—but a theme seldom explored—is its revelation of the writer's sense of community. What I seek to demonstrate in this essay is that Merton's poetry stands as a model of how a true monk does this in a seemingly paradoxical way through a quieting down and through an acceptance of self within his particular monastic way of life. There is no doubt that Thomas Merton's poetry is fundamentally a record of his personal encounter with the monastic life and its implications; yet as his career as a monk and a writer developed he seems to have become increasingly less concerned about himself as poet and even as a monk, and more so about the implications of what happens when one lives with, and for, others. Significantly, the later poetry finally reaches out to all the world.[1]

Late in his career Merton noted that a monk is one who takes up a critical attitude toward society in general. One of the facts which we encounter as we study Merton's poetry is that early as a cloistered monk-writer he often had to examine his desire to write and the fact of his public reputation. Initially, as a young monk, he wrote because of the vow of obedience. During those years he sometimes sought not to write, and wondered (in print) about the efficacy of writing: eventually he came around to the view that he could provide hints about the contemplative life for others. At the end of his third book of poetry, *Figures For an Apocalypse,* he chose to include a poem called "The Poet To His Book", in which he outlined some of his doubts about writing, but also his willingness to accept the mystery of God's plan which asked him to write while "silent". Such a poem is a protest about writing, yet it is also a statement of acceptance of the poet's vow of obedience and the role of the monastic poet. This poem is also a reflection of a willingness to follow directives for the greater good while the writer seems tortured that it would probably remain impossible for him to know if all of the correct decisions have been made. Above all, a poem like this one, which reflects doubts and ambiguities, reflects trust too. Maybe it is that quality more than any other which stands out in Merton's poetry as a whole. As a contemplative, he continued to raise questions, but his questions were raised within a context of trust and affirmation. The poetry as a whole is his record of a spiritual quest, an affirmation and journey, and while this was a journey marked by sideroads, occasional pauses, heights, even depressions, it remains a record of an intense conviction that this monk-writer was on his way.[2] The most important part of Merton would always continue to seek quiet; another part had to speak in, and through, the poetry. In "The Poet To His Book" he wrote:

> Go, stubborn talker,
> Find you a station on the loud world's corners.
> And try there, (if your hands be clean) your
>   length of patience:
> Use there the rhythms that upset my silence,
> And spend your pennyworth of prayer
> There in the clamour of the Christless avenues:
>
> And try to ransom some one prisoner
> Out of those walls of traffic, out of the wheels of
>   that unhappiness![3]

The body of Merton's poetry can be described as a gradual distillation of his experience of the monastic vocation; as we attain distance from the body of that work we see that it reflects the very journey which constituted his entire monastic life. His poems reflect a monk becoming surer of a role as contemplative—separated from other men so that he would be closer to God, yet paradoxically also closer to man.

There were many stages in Merton's journey; however the most important developments can be seen in four broad poetic movements. The first is a reflection of the years of the earliest monastic experience and formation, a time of his becoming accustomed to life in a monastery. During that period an enthusiasm for monastic observances is reflected and a manner which consciously reflects the rhythms of life within an enclosure can be distinguished. Later, Merton almost automatically incorporated such patterns into many poems, but he also became much more actively concerned about the very meaning of a cloister, and about persons outside the monastery. During the second period his conception of the monastic journey is changing, and a stronger compassion is reflected which is also found throughout the subsequent poetry. During still later periods, as Merton is becoming both more aware of the world of man, and of his own continuing need for solitude, concern about monastic observance seems to lessen. Lastly, in his final years we observe a burst of poetic production which is more difficult to characterize. Whereas the earliest poetry might be described as the reflection of a monk's embrace of the monastic life, the final poetic production is an embrace of all the world. Father Louis does this in many ways: through specific observations, through humor, through an awareness of the East, in examination of the nature of language, and through a bringing together of many things he read. This essay sketches the main outlines of these broad and often overlapping patterns, yet patterns clearly reflected in the poetry. First, as a young monk and poet Merton embraced tradition. Secondly, as communal life and trust became almost second nature, his enthusiasm for the religious life was absorbed into the poetry itself, yet many new themes also appear. This includes doubt. Thirdly, as Merton became more actively concerned about the relationship of the monastic life to the world, still other themes appeared. Lastly, when he was surest of his vocation, he could—in many ways which might before even have seemed surprising—celebrate all God's creation.

These broad movements are here vastly simplified, but I hope to show that Merton's poetry is a record of such a continuing journey. In his book, *Thoughts in Solitude* (1958), he wrote when a man stops asking how to live, and lives, then he has found his vocation.[4] Perhaps this is also what his poetry reveals. Merton accepted the traditions of the contemplative religious life; these traditions became second nature; he then could stand back from those traditions to raise questions. In so doing he was able both to bind himself more firmly to tradition, yet also continue alone on his solitary journey.

I

In Merton's early years as a monk he felt that the mystery of being enfolded in God's love was the crucial fact to be communicated; many of his earliest poems generated within the atmosphere of the Abbey of Gethsemani in Kentucky reflect this. It is almost as if this young writer could hardly believe that he found himself hidden in the rhythms of a disciplined monastic life. It is as if through God's mercy, and because of St Benedict's foresight, the young speaker had been delivered from a dead world. He suddenly found himself part of a living tradition. In his poem "Clairvaux", he sang of an earlier monastery whose spirit of community lived on in the Kentucky hills. In lines which echo Gerard Manley Hopkins, Merton writes of a sacred place and how its inhabitants support one another:

> O holy Bernard, wise in brotherlove,
> Vintner who train and grow, and prune and tie us
> Fast, trim us in sure and perfect arbors
>   of stability and rule:
> You have foreseen what vintages the Holy Spirit
>   Ripening, in our concord, as in vine-vein
>   the strong sun,
> Will trample in His press, His charity,
>   in the due day,
> To barrel us, His Burgundy.

> (*CP,* p. 128)

Because of monastic discipline, Gethsemani's monks also are the blood of Christ; this is possible because of the continuing atmosphere within the monastery. It is as if the building itself is alive:

> These arches live together
> Like psalms and antiphon[.]

(*CP*, p. 128)

Father Louis's image of strong simple architecture emphasizes the strengths of the communal life as he perceived it:

> My brothers, do you see these arches'
>   stones, how much they weigh,
> Yet how the leaning stress of charity
> Sports with weight, and laughs at height[?]

(*CP*, p. 128)

A related early poem is entitled "The Snare": and it is dedicated "for St Benedict, in thanksgiving". It is a prayer of deliverance, for the poet realizes that his earlier life had been one lived dangerously close to destruction:

> We planned our fortunes in an open trap.
> Led by our recklessness into the nets,
> Taking the bait, and slipping through the strings[.]

(*CP*, p. 97)

The implication is that through his community life which the *Rule* of St Benedict nurtures, life is now no longer fearful, but rather a joy. Merton seems to say life is protected because of the order of its daily routine. His Old Testament image of deliverance from the snare, and his trust reflected in the psalm-like chant of the poem emphasize the escape of the bird, and this poet's thankfulness, wonder, and awe.

Much of the early poetry tends toward such prayer and celebration; it reflects both the poet's contentment and historical awareness. "Trappists Working" serves as a model of what the young monk was experiencing. The poem is a lesson about working with others and it therefore reflects the communal spirit:

> Now all our saws sing holy sonnets in the world of timber
> Where oaks go off like guns, and fall like cataracts,
> Pouring their roar into the wood's green well.

Physical work unites the workers with nature, and this becomes a step toward Christ. Timbering is perceived as not different than other duties performed as part of the monastic routine; and in all such routine it is as if one can ask Jesus himself to participate in the actions:

> Walk to us, Jesus, through the walls of trees,
> And find us still adorers in these airy churches,
> Singing our other Office with our saws and axes.
> Still teach Your children in the busy forest,
> And let some little sunlight reach us, in
> our mental shades, and leafy studies.

(CP, p. 96)

The monk-writer knows that he should balance different activities and rituals. Too much activity, too much planning, too much trying to control will cause problems. (Many passages in *The Sign of Jonas* demonstrate this insight also).[5] What Merton seems to imply is that as monk he has to become part of a larger rhythm, but he also wonders if he should even think much about this, or try to put such experiences into poems. In the next broad movement within Merton's monastic journey we observe both his continuing ability to incorporate the rhythms of life within the monastery into the poetry, while at the same time there seems to be a growing discomfort because of questions raised about the practicability of even writing at all, and certainly about writing poetry.

Victor A. Kramer

II

 While it is true that Merton's poetry of the earliest monastic years is a song of praise which reflects enthusiasm and happiness, there is another strong element—something which includes both self-satisfaction and doubt—also present. This is partly so because while Merton was making strides during his first years as a cloistered monk, he also remained intensely aware of his role as writer situated between the life of the monastery and the world of his readers. Some of the poems produced during his early years in the monastery reflect his satisfaction with monastic life, yet perhaps almost too much concern with writing also is reflected. Some of these poems seem almost contrived; they are often extremely erudite, esoteric, even clever. (Merton himself recognized this fact when *Figures for an Apocalypse* was published).[6] The fact is he was struggling to reconcile his writing with his conception of the monastic vocation.

 In the years before he chose to enter the monastery Merton knew that ultimately he would have to choose between a public fame which at the time he desired, and a quieter kind of accomplishment never to be measured in public terms. Paradoxically, in a world literally obsessed with itself, it became Merton's vocation as a monk and writer to spell out what it meant to attempt to forget self in order to find union with God; this was a matter of insight, however, which came over a period of many years, insight sometimes mixed with pride in the creation of poems. The enthusiasm which the newly professed monk felt seems to have often been linked to the enthusiasm of the writer. This is evident throughout an important poem which he wrote in longhand for Mark Van Doren only a few days after his arrival at Gethsemani in late 1941. That poem is one of the earliest written after he had entered; it is called "A Letter to My Friend". It is a farewell note to friends who remained in the world, and a statement of the poet's realization of the promise of a monastic life, within, as he said:

This holy House of God,
Nazareth, where Christ lived as a boy,
These sheds and cloisters,
The very stones and beams are all befriended
By cleaner sun, by rarer birds, by
    lovelier flowers.

                                        (CP, pp. 90-91)

Merton's abbey is a special place where he, and his brother monks are nurtured in an atmosphere which will make them Christ-like. Yet it is almost as if this poet strives to make his image too otherworldly. Or, we might even assert, Merton desperately wants to be that way. While this young poet's dream of Gethsemani, as a kind of paradise, is understandable, it is hardly realistic. The reality of life day-by-day in a monastery is considerably different than Merton's conception at this point. Yet we could make a listing of other poems by the young monk which literally overflowed with such ideals.

Much of the earlier poetry employs a Gethsemani setting; it was as though the abbey itself spoke to this young monk. He was clearly fascinated with the beauty of this particular place. As time passed, however, he was to realize that it was not so much a matter of the particularities of walls and hills in Kentucky, or even of monastic ritual, but rather a matter of a way of being which allowed a monk to be disposed toward an awareness that could, indeed, should, develop anywhere. "After the Night Office—Gethsemani Abbey" suggests Merton's early attitudes. The darkest time of day seemed full of light because mysteriously God's word illumined the very atmosphere of one particular place:

It is not yet the grey and frosty time
When barns ride out of the night like ships:
We do not see the Brothers, bearing lanterns,
Sink in the quiet mist,
As various as the spirits who, with lamps, are sent

> To search our souls' Jerusalems
> Until our houses are at rest
> And minds enfold the Word, our Guest.
>
> (*CP*, p. 108)

The poet searches for striking images which illuminate the darkness of which he sings. Many of these patterns of images, and especially those of light and darkness, seem to be derived from the psalms. This poem continues:

> Praises and canticles anticipate
> Each day the singing bells that wake the sun.
> But now our psalmody is done.
> Our hasting souls outstrip the day:
> Now, before dawn, they have their noon.
> The Truth that transubstantiates the body's night
> Has made our minds His temple-tent:
> Open the secret eye of faith
> And drink these deeps of invisible light.
>
> (*CP*, pp. 108-109)

At such times we have the feeling that perhaps this poet is trying too hard to impress us with his comprehension of the monk's paradoxical situation. Similarly, the poem "The Dark Encounter" is one where he sings of "silence with no syllable for weapon" (*CP*, 112). While these poems, are valuable they remain rather abstract. Later poems, which deal rather more specifically with the experience of Gethsemani, seem to say more about the particulars of the monastic journey. Like God's grace, such insight and poetry came unbidden. One poem about a monastery's barn fire, a surprise and a paradoxical sign, is an example of Father Louis learning to find such poetry, not producing it.

Just as the monastery, and other monks served as inspiration for Merton the poet, his reading and study blossomed forth too. This also apparently went through a process of change. There are the early exemplary poems about Clairvaux, and about St John the Baptist, about St Jerome and St Paul the Hermit, Rievaulx, and St Aelred. Many of these are excellent, but again (to generalize) they can at times seem contrived. What Merton, as monk and poet, needed was time, experience, and the particulars of knowing individuals who would help him to make connections between abstractions about monastic history and its living continuity in the present. As a poet he came to see that insights about the monastic journey could be made in many ways which were not so overtly "monastic", liturgical, or biblical. His poem "The Blessed Virgin Compared to a Window" suggests the stance of the earlier period. She is the model:

> Because my will is simple as a window
> And knows no pride of original earth,
> It is my life to die, like glass, by light:
> Slain in the strong rays of the bridegroom sun.

> (*CP,* p. 46)

Likewise, several poems about St John the Baptist could be cited. Many of these are technical accomplishments, yet precisely because they are such clever accomplishments, one sometimes wonders if they were not (as Merton himself suspected in his essay entitled "Poetry and Contemplation") more distractions than guideposts in his journey toward God.

In still other early poems he records what it was like to realize that the saints and biblical passages were significant models. They apparently showed him what he needed to do, and through such exemplification, he was to be strengthened in the religious life. Yet this remained a life which Merton, as poet, seemed to revel in to some degree because of its separation from persons outside the monastery, maybe even because of the separation from others within the monastery. In some of these poems there is a quality which almost suggests smugness about the wonder and awe which Merton states is inexpressible and which he labors so hard to express. (Part of what seems to

121

be occurring is that he continues to write to convince himself of his vocation as monk.)

In later, usually less self-conscious, poems Merton developed a different awareness of monasticism along with growing awareness of others. Simultaneously, it should be noted, his concern with the "success" of his writing diminished. There are, it should be noted, not absolute successive stages in Merton's writing or in this reflection of his monastic career, for already during his earliest years as monk he was learning how to focus on the immediate and to forget self. In his early poems about fields, trees, and the weather of Kentucky, poems which celebrate the particularities of place, he was already learning to be content with the immediate. He knew that others who had gone before him had learned such lessons. Those monks were his models and his poem "The Trappist Cemetery—Gethsemani" becomes, therefore, a prayer for all the men who sleep in the cemetery which he saw daily. This is a poem about simplicity, but it also remains a statement by a young poet about his ability to make clever poems. The cemetery is imagined in striking comparisons: the old monks have completed their voyage; this comparison generates another:

> And we, the mariners, and travellers,
> The wide-eyed immigrants,
> Praying and sweating in our steerage cabins
> Lie still and count with love the measured bells
> That tell the deep-sea leagues until your harbor.
>
> (*CP,* p. 117)

Simultaneously, we think this moving, even powerful; yet we cannot help but realize it is rather literary. Merton informs us of the quiet monastic journey, but he reminds us of his poetic imagination as well. Significantly, in later poems he ceased being very much concerned with the intricacy of his poetic imagination as something to be displayed.

III

The third broad pattern reflected in Merton's poetry goes beyond the blended enthusiasm, self-satisfaction, and doubt which has been outlined for Merton came to realize that no monastic journey was ever to be expressed through words, or completed through formulas. A monk's real journey, his poems seem to say more and more during the middle years, is one toward simplicity, certainly not literary sophistication. Yet it also is a matter of realizing that those who are living alone are part of the Body of Christ. It is for such reasons that he chose as epigraph for *The Tears of Blind Lions,* (1949), a sentence from Leon Bloy "When those who love God try to talk about him, their words are blind lions looking for springs in the desert".

In years which immediately followed in the early nineteen-fifties, his questioning period, Merton's poetic subjects became far more specific. We should remember, he had already by this time absorbed the rhythm of the choir. Now it seemed as if he could write his own psalms:

> When psalms surprise me with their music
> And antiphons turn to rum
> The Spirit sings: The bottom drops out of my soul
>
> And from the center of my cellar, Love,
>   louder than thunder
> Opens a heaven of naked air.

(CP, p. 220)

The point is that when this happens, one finds poems everywhere, even in the quietest and most unliterary kinds of places:

> I drink rain, drink wind
> Distinguishing poems
> Boiling up out of the cold forest.

(CP, p. 197)

Strange to say, what seems to be occurring is that while many of these poems sound as if they had been informed by the very rhythm of the choir, what the monk expresses is that the superficial routines of the monastery are becoming of far less importance for him. His "A Responsory, 1948" and "Freedom as Experience" document such a change. What he is telling readers is that finding God is to find oneself alone, even while perhaps place does help.

One way Merton the poet becomes more aware of his deepest need is through close observation of the simplest facts of nature and through observation of details of living which he might not have even noticed in earlier circumstances. It then becomes possible to sing songs within the simplest set of circumstances. The support of others saying the Office, or meeting in the chapter room remains important, but all this also makes it possible to be quiet and to take refreshment in ways which might have earlier seemed surprising:

> Thus I live on my own land, on my own island
> And speak to God, my God, under the doorway
> When rain, (sings light) rain has devoured my house
> And winds wade through my trees.
>
> (*CP*, p. 197)

The monk learns to be alone, and he learns that God then comes in ways which are surprising.

Two poems, which seem at first contradictory, but are in fact complementary reveal a considerable amount about this poet's changing views concerning the contemplative vocation during a time when he also raised many questions about the monastic life. One is an admonition, "To a Severe Nun"; the other is entitled "Elias—Variations on a Theme". The first is a poem of admonition to a nun who, Merton's speaker imagines, will try to seek God through pain and denial, "a path too steep for others to follow" (*CP*, p. 287). Such violence, he insists, is an evasion. What he implies is that God speaks in all kinds of ways, yet we can easily not hear, especially if we are too much concerned with our own activities. To enter fully into a religious life we must be open to God's voice—not to our own manipulations. (It is not an exaggeration to say that Merton was coming to similar conclusions about his own poetic production.) Thus, "To a Severe Nun" condemns any member of a religious order who would seek to find God without the help of others. One cannot do it oneself. And then, on the other hand, one learns to simplify.

"Elias—Variations on a Theme" celebrates the fact of God's coming under circumstances which one would not ordinarily expect, and precisely at the time when one stops trying too hard. Merton implies that until we are willing to listen, we will not hear. Could it have been, he suggests, that his earliest poetry was too full of itself?

> And I have been a man without silence,
> A man without patience, with too many
> Questions.
>
> . . . .
>   Under the blunt pine
> Elias becomes his own geography . . . .
>
> (*CP*, 243 & 245)

Merton's long poem, "Elias", may be the most important single poem of his monastic career. In it he stresses that while there is a beauty in any individual's enterprise

> The free man does not float
> On the tides of his own expedition.

As he became able to write more poems like the "Elias—Variations", Merton was also less interested in writing which appeared to be proud of its accomplishments, puffed up with a sense of accomplishment. Significantly this lessening of self-consciousness opened up another whole realm.

IV

It must be correct to say that Merton (as monk and poet) became *both* surer and less sure of the benefits of communal life and writing about it. (We remember all his "temptations" over the years to become a Carthusian, to become a hermit, etc.). He was apparently during those years coming to realize that the externals of the monastic life were only externals, yet he was also sure of his own monastic vocation. Its routine, its rhythms, even its frustrations, had become part of his being closer to God. The question, of course, had become how to communicate such facts—especially when few people read poetry, and also when the glamour of the monastic life is dimmed. One way is through a simplification, both in subject matter and technique. There are numerous examples of this in poems written during the final years of Merton's career.

While Merton sought to express an extreme simplification, he also saw that the world was inundated by too much seeing and hearing which made it almost impossible to see and to hear. It was precisely for such reasons that during his last three years (when he was living as a hermit) he devised the radical experiments of *Cables to the Ace.* Technology, complexity, cleverness had made it impossible to appreciate the simplicities of what earlier visionaries had seen: "The sayings of the saints are put away in air-conditioned archives" (*CP,* p. 396). Yet even though that is the case, and while man chooses to shroud himself with language that is meaningless, God's grace still comes. The monk–poet writes:

> Slowly, slowly,
> Comes Christ through the ruins[.]

> (*CP,* p. 449)

Merton as solitary, sought ways to remind contemporary man to simplify. In some poems, for example, he returned to the legends of earlier times. "Macarius and the Pony" stresses a simplicity of spirit through a legend about villagers who imagined evil. Macarius speaks to them:

> "Your own eyes
> (Said Macarius)
> Are your enemies.
> Your own crooked thoughts
> (Said the anchorite)
> Change people around you[.]

(*CP*, 318)

Likewise, a poem called "Song for Nobody" stresses the need for simplification:

> A yellow flower
> (Light and spirit)
> Sings by itself
> For nobody.

(*CP*, 337)

In another related poem Merton reminds us that a night-flowering cactus is its true self "Only in the dark". In such poems he hints that a simplicity of approach was the real key in man's journey to God. And we must assume that is what he learned as monk. It is only through silence that the word can bloom. This is summed up in "Love Winter When the Plant Says Nothing", and, as well, in many of the poems which Merton translated from the Chinese of Chuang Tzu.[7]

It is significant that concurrent with Merton's development of a sureness about the contemplative vocation he also wrote many more poems which went back to the world. It was as if the silence and discipline and insight of being alone provided a clearer vision of a world which refused to be alone and therefore denied itself a true vision of God's universe. But suddenly everything makes sense if one can achieve a proper perspective, the poet indicates:

> Slowly Slowly
> Christ rises on the cornfields . . . .
>
> (*CP,* p. 449)

> The sound of the earth goes up to embrace
>   the constant sky.
> My own center is the teeming heart of natural families.
>
> (*CP,* p. 443)

Cables to the Ace, the book from which the preceding quotations come, could, it seems, only have been written by a monk who, in his compassion, knew that all men desperately need the quiet and solitude which is the monk's daily feast. But how could Merton tell his fellowmen to let go? How could he speak of Eckhart's *Gelassenheit* when all the world seems to be holding on to insignificant things, words, sounds, rituals? This poet, who earlier tried so hard, now knows:

> Once you become aware of
> yourself as seeker, you are
> lost. But if you are content
> to be lost you will be
> found without knowing it,
> precisely because you are
> lost, for you are, at last,
> nowhere.
>
> (*CP,* p. 452)

An attitude of joyousness accounts for much of Merton's final poetry, finally an imaginative journey to all parts of the world, combined with a monastic commentary about the need for simplicity.

Greater tolerance, flexibility, openness, these became the key toward the end of his poetic career. We see this in many specific ways in the later poetry. Only a few specific examples of this broad pattern—all of which might be examined in far more detail will be provided. First, Father Louis' broadening concern for others is reflected in many of his later occasional poems. Secondly, toward the end of his career a sense of humor became more obvious, even in a poem as complex as *The Geography of Lograire.* Lastly, his renditions of psalms composed towards the end of his career help us to see his simplicity and his compassion. His mature translations of the psalms and other passages from the Old Testament are in language which people beyond the monastery easily appreciate.

In the final phase of his poetic production compassion and concern for others is basic. Poems about Hiroshima, about concentration camps, about refugees, about civil rights workers, about one's contemporaries who are inundated by material goods—all these are Merton's subjects. One of the reasons he could assume such a wide range of interests was because he no longer took the monastic world of the Cistercians quite as seriously as he did when he first had entered the monastery. During these final years he could write of the simplicity of a flower, or a child, and at the same time he could laugh with his fellow monks.

Still another important characteristic of Merton's mature poetry is that as he achieved distance from the daily life of a monk, and from the world, he could stress humorous aspects of all living. As he had become surer of his own monastic vocation he could laugh about aspects of community life, for example, the extremely profitable cheese-making. (His poem entitled "CHEE$E" is spelled with a dollar sign.) And his "A Practical Program for Monks" is a gentle commentary about what can happen when there is too much emphasis put upon rules and regulations. "A Practical Program" reflects Merton laughing at rules and usages which can be pushed out of all proportion. It is an exaggeration, but essentially correct to assert that his final book *The Geography of Lograire* is an investigation of a related topic. By 1967-1968 when this book was being written, Merton clearly realized that we see things because of our bias. If men could see the humor of it, then we might be willing to both laugh *and* be willing to see the tragedy which is western history. In *The Geography of Lograire* he demonstrates what happens when western man takes his own personal interpretation of history too rigidly, and in the process forgets about others.

The Geography of Lograire is Merton's affirmation of trust in God, but it is as well sometimes an almost surreal nightmare of western man's manipulation of facts for his own selfish gain. Merton's job as poet was to show readers how the myth-dream of any people can be easily distorted and misunderstood if a framework from a dominant culture is superimposed on a less aggressive, or economically successful, or technologically advanced culture. Writing from the perspective of a monk who had learned the need to respect others and not to impose frameworks, but also the need to speak out, Merton's poem is considerably different than his earlier poetry of monastic awe. Wonder, awe, amazement are still basic, but it also became a matter of saying no one should be smug about where he stands, or trades, or prays.

Perhaps the most important thing Merton reminds western man of in *The Geography of Lograire* is that too narrow a view of history can only result in distortion. On the other hand, tolerance places one's own perspective in proper relation to the developing history of a world given to all men by God.

Another example of Merton's concern with placing things in a broader perspective—is the group of psalms which he rendered into the vernacular during his last years. His respect for the psalms is delineated in his study *Bread in the Wilderness;*[8] there he emphasizes a fascination with the psalms as a living continuity with the past. His late translations stress connections with the present moment. I mention these poems since they serve to illustrate how this monk who could earlier almost ridicule "the world" had in maturity developed an important compassion for mankind. Similarly, his verses for Jonas (Chapter 2), entitled "All the Way Down", constitute a poem which is both about Jonas *and* what it means to be rejected in today's world.

What is clear throughout the final phase of Merton's poetic production—whether through compassionate poems, humorous ones, translations, or even in the esoteric lines of *Lograire*—is that he came more and more to appreciate the particularities of each life. Even within a monastery, he often implies, while it is seemingly covered over by traditions so that the exterior of many lives seemed the same, each person is most importantly an individual.

In conclusion, I mention a poem which Father Louis wrote for one of his Trappist brothers. This spontaneously composed "Elegy for a Trappist" was posted on the community bulletin board the day Father Stephen died. It reflects the poet's admiration for a simple old monk, who has been a gardener, and it reflects the journey Merton himself made perhaps better than any further theorizing. It is a poem which is, just as the earliest Merton, enthusiastic about the religious life, but this elegy is a very particular portrait of one man, not an abstract model. This is the real change. Merton's elegy is a poem which is successful because he refuses to rely upon formulas, or upon witty phrasing; the poet refuses to let the poet step forward; yet he clearly remains fascinated with the particulars of what he sees. Father Stephen made the successful journey, and Merton tells us he did so by going nowhere; he did so through specific acts of love, hiding his bouquets, but nevertheless changing the very atmosphere. Merton's poems communicate some of this same mystery.

Dorothy LeBeau

THE SOLITARY LIFE

Introduction

Thomas Merton wrote a poem about the desert cactus whose flower is rarely seen as it opens only once and then in darkness. The petals of the flower are a pearly white with a waxen quality; its heart is a deep nest of gold filaments that finely curl with a foam-like texture. Surrounded by a golden stalk which rises out of the flower like a clarion horn it lives in silence and blooms in secret.[1] This poem describes Merton's vocation in solitude, searching for God and his true self in the purifying, yet illuminating darkness of dread, poverty, mystery and transformation. He shares that journey with us, but as he wrote in the "Night-Flowering Cactus":

> I know my time, which is obscure, silent and brief
> For I am present without warning one night only.

> When sun rises on the brass valleys I become serpent.

Though I show my true self only in the dark and to
    no man
(For I appear by day as serpent)
I belong neither to night nor day.

Sun and city never see my deep white bell
Or know my timeless moment of void:
There is no reply to my munificence.

When I come to life my sudden Eucharist
Out of the earth's unfathomable joy

Clean and total I obey the world's body
I am intricate and whole, not art but wrought passion
Excellent deep pleasures of essential waters
Holiness of form and mineral mirth:

I am the extreme purity of virginal thirst.

I neither show my truth nor conceal it
My innocence is decried dimly
Only by divine gift
As a white cavern without explanation.

He who sees my purity
Dares not speak of it.
When I open once for all my impeccable bell
No one questions my silence:
The all-knowing bird of night flies out of my mouth.

Have you seen it? Then though my mirth has
    quickly ended
You live forever in its echo:
You will never be the same again.[2]

This poem of transformation, the discovery of one's true

identity in Christ, expresses for Merton, in symbolic language, his relationship with God and contemporary men and women. He was called, as he wrote, "to be what I am, a man seeking God in silence and solitude, with deep respect for the demands and realities of their own vocation, and fully aware that others are seeking the truth in their own way".[3]

Merton lived in solitude and silence because he sought to be one with God in love and contemplation. For Merton contem-✶ plation is the intuitive awakening of one's whole life existentially and consciously to the presence of God, in communion with Him, in Christ, through the Holy Spirit. In the conscious awareness of this relationship of love the false self is annihilated and the true self emerges as one is transformed. The realization of one's true identity is to become perfectly like God; it is God living in God, seeing God as God sees, loving as God loves—with His compassion.

The study of the solitary life of Thomas Merton which follows, includes a biographical sketch of his movement into greater solitude, a review of the influences of his thought— biblical, patristic and monastic, dimensions expressive of the hermit life including solitude and silence, poverty, sitting alone in the cell for the Name of God, and love and union with God in Christ. In addition, the discovery of the true self in the solitude of contemplation, the diminishment of the false self, and the human person created in the image and restored to the likeness of God are illustrated.

A Biographical Survey

Thomas Merton, born of artist parents in France in 1915, orphaned at age fifteen, educated in France, England and the United States, and converted to Roman Catholicism at twenty-three, entered the Cistercian Monastery of Our Lady of Gethsemani on December 10, 1941. For the next twenty-seven years, as a monk, priest, Master of Scholastics, Master of Novices, author, poet, spiritual director, fire warden, and in the last three years of his life, as a hermit, Merton searched for God and his true identity in Christ. As such, his journey was a movement into deeper silence and solitude. He describes this life of contemplation and identifies it as his own in a message sent to the Synod of Bishops meeting in Rome in October 1967:

> The contemplative life has nothing to tell you except to reassure you and say that if you dare to penetrate your own silence and dare to advance without fear into the solitude with the lonely other who seeks God through you and with you, then you will truly recover the light and capacity to understand what is beyond words and beyond explanations because it is too close to be explained: it is the <u>intimate union in the depths of your own heart, of God's spirit and your own secret inmost self</u>, so that you and He are in <u>truth one spirit</u>.[4]

Merton searched for unity, and his love and desire for union with God, self and others led him into the solitude of the hermitage. While he initially characterizes this solitude as related to contemplation, after living as a hermit he expresses it in more dynamic, social, ecumenical and universal terms.

The beginning of the movement into solitude can be discerned in Merton's earliest monastic works. In these, Merton reveals himself as one who could be very much his own company, while, at the same time, could communicate in a warm and disarming friendliness and affection.[5] In *The Seven Storey Mountain* he writes of solitary travels in France, Germany and Italy, of walks in the woods surrounding St Bonaventure's, and of the Kentucky knobs which he explored, and it is in the last paragraphs of his autobiography that he shares his life-long desire for solitude.[6] He discovers that <u>it is God who leads him into solitude</u>. The path is one of poverty, reduction, abandonment, detachment, loneliness, of being driven into the desert, of flight from pleasures and gifts, of rejection, mystery, faith and of death in Christ. And yet it also leads to the high places of joy and mercy, it will bear fruit in the souls of others, and through anguish and poverty, it is becoming the brother of God and growing in knowledge of Christ with those who have been faithful to the same journey.

In the early days of Merton's monastic vocation, this journey is characterized by the desire for solitude that emerges as a need for quiet for prayer; he describes this solitude as difficult to find in a large and flourishing monastery. Eight years after his entrance into the monastery, in 1949, Merton understands more of solitude. He relates:

> And now, for the first time I began to know what it means to be alone. Before becoming a priest I had made a great fuss about solitude and had been rather a nuisance to my superiors and directors in my aspirations for a solitary life. Now, after my ordination, I discovered that the essence of a solitary vocation is that it is a vocation to fear, to helplessness, to isolation in the invisible God. Having found this, I now began for the first time in my life to taste a happiness that was so complete and so profound that I no longer had any need to remind myself that I was happy . . . . [7]

Merton discovers another dimension of solitude when he becomes the Master of Scholastics in 1951; he speaks of the scholastics in the solitude he has recognized within himself. He observes:

> The best of them, and the ones to whom I feel closest, are also the most solitary . . . All this experience replaces my theories of solitude. I do not need a hermitage, because I have found one where I least expected it. It was when I knew my brothers less well that my thoughts were more involved with them. Now that I know them better, I can see

> something of the depths of solitude which are in
> every human person, but which most men do not
> lay open either to themselves or to God.[8]

Early in 1955 Merton again struggles with his desire to
embrace the eremetical life. He applies to the Congregation of
Religious in Rome for permission to transfer to the Camaldolese.[9] While waiting for the decision to be made he writes to
Dom Jean Leclercq:

> If God wants me to be a solitary, I will be His kind
> of solitary, no matter what may be the exterior
> conditions that may be imposed on me. Of this, I am
> certain, and I am beginning to find that as time goes
> on I do become, inevitably more of a solitary, and
> that the very moves that destroy my tending into
> solitude have the effect of making me interiorly—and
> even exteriorly—more of a hermit. Why, then, should
> I worry much about what is to be done?[10]

Merton was denied permission to transfer to the Camaldolese
and late in the same year until 1965 became the Master of
Novices. About this development he comments, "I have the
disadvantage of a strong attraction to the woods and to solitude, and I suppose that it would spoil everything if my desires
were fulfilled. But I shall still be in charge of the forest and take
the novices out to fell trees and plant in the spring".[11]

The desire for more perfect solitude is fulfilled for Thomas
Merton on August 29, 1965 when he began his hermit life in a
cinderblock cabin, on a wooded hill, not far from the monastery. He writes:

> . . . this week I officially begin the hermit life . . .
> and I am all set to go . . . . It is quite a step, and
> something that has not been done officially in the
> Order, since the Lord knows when, way back in

the Middle Ages, when we had a few hermit saints. I hope I will follow in their footsteps (sanely however).[12]

Merton lived in the hermitage until October 1968, approximately three years before his death in Asia.

Influences Regarding the Solitary Life

It is within the tradition of the Roman Catholic Church and the Cistercian Order that Merton views the hermit life; he was influenced by three major sources—biblical, patristic and monastic.

"It seems to me", Merton articulates, "that the solitary contemplative life is an imitation and fulfillment in ourselves of these words of Jesus: 'The Son can do nothing of himself, but only what He sees the Father doing. For whatever he does, this the Son also does in like manner. For the Father loves the Son and shows him all that he himself does'" (John 5:19-20). He continues:

> This imitation consists in being and acting in the same relation to Jesus as Jesus to the Father (John 5:24). "He who hears my word, and believes him who sent me, has life everlasting . . . " (John 6:44-45). "Everyone who has listened to the Father and has learned, comes to me". We listen to the Father best in solitude. Jesus is the Bread of Life given to us in solitude. "As the living Father has sent me, and as I live because of the Father, so he who eats me, he also shall live because of me" (John 6:58).[13]

It is in solitude that the hermit grows in receptivity to the Word of the Father, and therein receives the nourishment of Jesus. This receptivity leads the solitary into abandonment and poverty.

The complete dependence and abandonment of the hermit

to God is the proper stance of the hermit. Merton counsels, "From his first day in solitude, the hermit should set his heart upon understanding how to afflict his whole being with tears and desire before God. Then he will be like Daniel, to whom the angel brought God's answer. 'Fear not Daniel: for from the first day that thou didst set thy heart to understand, to afflict thyself in the sight of thy God, thy words have been heard . . . . ' " (cf. Daniel 10:12).[14]

As a hermit, the monk, led by the Spirit, follows Jesus into the desert so that he might engage in combat with the devil; this struggle is the prelude of the one in the Garden of Gethsemani. Merton explains:

> It is here, (the hermitage) in this inexpressible rending of his own poverty, that the hermit enters, like Christ, into the arena where he wages the combat that can never be told to anyone. This is the battle that is seen by no one except God, and whose vicissitudes are so terrible that when the victory comes at last, the total poverty and emptiness of the victor are so absolute that there is no longer any place in his heart for pride.[15]

The early models who followed Jesus into the desert, and who greatly influenced Merton, were the first Christian hermits of the fourth century. According to him, what the Fathers sought most ardently was their own true selves in Christ. He elaborates:

> The Desert Father . . . could not dare risk attachment to his own ego, or the dangerous ecstasy of self-will. He could not retain the slightest identification with his superficial, transient, self-constructed self. He had to lose himself in the inner, hidden reality of a self that was transcendent, mysterious, half known, and lost in Christ. He had to die to the values of

transient existence as Christ had died to them on the Cross, and rise from the dead with Him in the light of an entirely new wisdom. Hence the life of sacrifice, which started out from a clean break, separating the monk from the world. A life continued in "compunction" which taught him to lament the madness of attachment to unreal values. A life of solitude and labor, poverty and fasting, charity and prayer which enabled the old superficial self to be purged away and permitted the gradual emergence of the true secret self in which the believer and Christ were "one Spirit".[16]

However, he cautions, that " . . . to merely reproduce the simplicity, austerity, and prayer of these primitive souls is not a complete or satisfactory answer for those who would today seek the hermit life".[17] The hermit of today is called to transcend all who have gone before in embracing contemplative solitude which would relax, heal and soothe out the distortions and inhumanities of the twentieth century person.

The *Rule* of St Benedict provided Merton with the monastic affirmation of the valid transition from the cenobium to the hermitage as it states:

> . . . there are anchorites or hermits who have come through the test of living in a monastery for a long time, and have passed beyond the first fervor of monastic life. Thanks to the help and guidance of many, they are now trained to fight against the devil. They have built up their strength and go from the battle line in the ranks of their brothers to the single combat of the desert. Self-reliant now, without support of another, they are ready with God's help to grapple single-handed with the vices of body and mind.[18]

This period of transition described by Benedict is essential for the proper training and testing of the monk who moved from the monastery to the solitude of caves, wilderness, valleys and clefts of rocks.

The problem faced by Merton in regard to this transition, even though it was described in the *Rule,* was the historical Cistercian emphasis on cenobitism prevalent since the time of Bernard. In response to the denial or underestimation of the eremetical vocation Merton believed that the hermit life was recognized and respected in the Church as the normal fulfillment of the monastic state, though not always connected with it. In addition he warned that, "If the cenobium disdains and repudiates the hermitage it dooms itself to mediocracy. When the windows of the monastery no longer open out upon the vast horizons of the desert the monastic community inevitably becomes immersed in vanity".[19] Thus the life of more perfect solitude completed both the cenobium and the hermitage.

The Solitary Life

It is in the integration of biblical, patristic, and monastic sources and personal experience that Merton grows in understanding the vocation of the hermit as a call into solitude and silence in Christ. He articulates:

> Like everything else in the Christian life, the vocation to solitude can be understood only within the perspective of God's mercy to man in the incarnation of Christ. If there is any such thing as a Christian hermit, then he must be a man who has a special function in the mystical body of Christ—a hidden and spiritual function, and perhaps all the more vital because more hidden.[20]

The one who responds to the solitary vocation does so as one personally called by God in Christ. Thus the life is necessarily characterized by love for God, and is based on faith in silence. It is in solitude that faith is actualized, and one is enabled to accept responsibility for one's interior life in the mysterious presence of God. This commitment is made in loneliness, silence and the incomprehensible call to transcendence. Merton expresses his image of the journey into solitude and silence in the poem

Song: If You Seek . . .

> If you seek a heavenly light
> I Solitude am your professor
>
> I go before you in emptiness
> Raise strange suns for your new mornings,
> Opening the windows
> Of your innermost apartment.
>
> When I, loneliness, give my special signal
> Follow my silence, follow where I beckon!
> Fear not, little beast, little spirit
> (Thou word and animal)
> I solitude am angel
> And have prayed your name.
> . . . .
> Follow my ways and I will lead you
> To golden-haired suns,
> Logos and music, blameless joys,
> Innocent of questions
> And beyond answers:
>
> For I, Solitude, am thine own self:
> I, nothingness, am thy All
> I, Silence, am thy Amen![21]

Silence and solitude, terms which Merton tends to use synonymously, define complementary dimensions of one

143

reality. At the deepest level of oneself they unite so closely and are almost inseparable. At this level of mysterious interior solitude the soul is absorbed in the immense and fruitful silence of God, a silence and solitude which are infinite.[22] Such an absorption in the silence and solitude of God implies an emptiness in the soul. The one who longs to be led by the professor of solitude embarks upon a journey which opens into the abyss of the soul. Merton details:

> The only way to find solitude is by hunger and thirst and sorrow and poverty and desire, and the man who has found solitude is empty, as if he has been emptied by death.
> He has advanced beyond all horizons. There are not directions left in which he can travel. This is a country whose center is everywhere and whose circumference is nowhere. You do not find it by traveling but by standing still.[23]

In hunger and thirst, sorrow and poverty, and with desire, the hermit has, as his most important obligation to "sit in his cell", in the tradition of the Desert Fathers. The most important ascetic practice is solitude itself and sitting alone in the silence of the cell; this waiting in faith brings one into direct confrontation with the baffling mystery of God.

The one who sits in the cell does so for the Name of God. One is called into solitude to encounter the Name which is present and waiting in one's own place. ". . . the Name becomes, as it were, a cell within a cell, an inner spiritual cell. When I am in the cell or its immediate environs, I should recognize that I am 'where the Name of God dwells', and that living in the presence of this great Name I gradually become the one He wills me to be".[24]

The hermit who sits in his cell in the transforming presence of God is acutely aware of his spiritual poverty. In expressing the depths of this poverty, Merton reveals that it penetrates even the life of prayer and he writes of the impoverished one:

> . . . you would think that in his solitude he would
> quickly reach the level of visions, of mystical
> marriage, something dramatic at any rate. Yet he
> may well be poorer than the cenobite, even *in his life
> of prayer*. His is a weak and precarious existence, he
> has to struggle to preserve himself from all kinds of
> petty annoyances, and often fails to do so. His poverty
> is spiritual. It invades his whole soul as well as his
> body, and in the end his whole patrimony is one of
> insecurity. He enjoys the sorrow, the spiritual and
> intellectual indigence of the really poor. Obviously
> such a vocation has in it a grain of folly.[25]

The utter poverty of the solitary may result in an incapacity
to pray, to see, to hope. Indeed, the full extent of his contemplation may be manifested by a doubt that questions the very
root of his existence and undermines his reasons for existing
and for doing what he does. This doubt, of which Merton
speaks, is that which reduces one to a silence that asks no
questions, with a certitude of the presence of God only in
uncertainty and nothingness. The paradox of this uncertainty
and nothingness, however, is that the solitary " . . . generally
has peace. He is happy, but he never has a good time. He knows
where he is going, but he is not 'sure of his way', he just knows
he is going there".[26]

The solitude and peace that the hermit discovers is rooted in
the existence of Love. Above all else the life of the solitary is
lived in this Love.

> . . . in solitude one *is* at the root (of existence). He
> who is alone, and is conscious of what his solitude
> means, finds himself in the ground of life. He is
> 'in Love'. He is in love with all, with everyone,
> with everything. He is not surprised at this, and is

145

> able to love with this disconcerting and unexciting
> reality, which has no explanation. He lives, then, as
> a seed planted in the ground. As Christ said, the
> seed in the ground must die. To be as a seed in the
> ground of one's very life is to dissolve in that
> ground in order to become fruitful. One disappears
> into Love, in order to "be Love". But this fruitful-
> ness is beyond any planning and any understanding
> of man. To be "fruitful" in this sense, one must
> forget every idea of fruitfulness or productivity, and
> merely *be*.[27]

The hermit lives in the will of God in which productivity
or practicality are not measured and one disappears and is
hidden in the freedom of one who simply is.

To be, in Love and Unity: this is the one thing necessary for
the Christian hermit. Solitude, silence, poverty, sitting in one's
cell for the Name of God are embraced for the sake of living in
love in union with God in Christ. Merton clearly relates the
ultimate importance of union with Christ in the eremetical
vocation:

> . . . if the eremetical life is the highest form of
> Christianity it is because the hermit aspires more
> than anyone else to perfect union with Christ. Jesus
> Himself is the living Rule of the hermit, just as he
> is the model of every religious. It is Christ Himself
> who calls us into solitude . . . . Perhaps more than
> any other the solitary life demands the presence of
> the Man Christ who lives and suffers in us . . . . [28]

The hermit is called to live in union with Christ; and is able
to do so as one naturally created in the image and likeness of
God. In one's creation the human person is given a natural
tendency of being drawn to God in perfect identification and
a capacity for perfect freedom and pure love. " . . . at the very

146

core of our essence we are created in God's likeness in our freedom and in the exercise of that freedom . . . the exercise of disinterested love; the love of God for His own sake—because He
is God".[29]

Although united by nature the human person has, in a sense,
failed to realize this fundamental orientation to God. That
which is most natural has been weakened by original sin and,
consequently, natural union with the Divine Image is inaccessi-
ble and cannot be actualized without grace. Fallen humanity
has retained the image of God, although it has been disfigured,
but has lost likeness to God. The image of God is distorted by
"unlikeness".[30]

The problem of unlikeness is that the human person has
become deeply false and alienated from the inmost reality of
the true or inner self one was meant to be, made in the image
of God. However, Merton reflects;

> The image of God in man—the openness to love, the
> capacity for total consent to God in himself and in
> others—remains indestructible. But it can be buried
> and imprisoned under selfishness. The image of God
> in man is not destroyed by sin but utterly disfigured
> by it. To be exact, the image of God in man becomes
> contradictory when its openness closes in upon it-
> self, when it ceases to be a capacity for love and
> simply an appetite for dominion or possession . . . .[31]

It is Christ that calls the human person to transformation and
the restoration of the capacity for freedom and love in mystical
or transforming union, a higher, more intimate union than
natural union. Transforming union represents the perfect incorporation of the human person to Christ in loving faith. This
becoming in perfection implies dynamic growth and development to increasingly more perfect and complete union with the
risen Christ, and communion with Him in perfect love. In this
transformation one is progressively called to respond to the goal

vocation of transforming union with Christ

for which one is created—to become perfectly conformed to the likeness of Christ.[32]

God calls the Christian to transforming union, and in being conformed to the likeness to Christ, to the conscious awareness of that union. In the discovery of the presence of God within, one also discovers the true self. The discovery of the true self implies that one comes to the realization that one's true identity is not that which appears on the surface. This false, exterior, superficial, social self is made up of prejudices, whimsy, posturing, pharisaic self-concern and pseudo dedication.[33] The false self is a human construct built by selfishness and flights from reality, and because it is not of God, is substantially empty and incapable of experiencing the love and freedom of God.

The false superficial self dies and is forgotten in solitude, as the true self comes to full maturity. This true self cannot be possessed, acquired or attained, and can only be and act according to the deeper laws of God. In solitude the true self shares in the solitude and loneliness of God and others and the hermit learns to face illusion, to resist temptation and to pray. One is forced to face the nothingness, limitation and infidelity of one's own life and is purified and enabled to maturely give oneself authentically in love.

The Christian solitary is completely devoted, in loving concentration, to the conscious awareness of transforming union with Christ, the death of the false self and the emergence of one's true identity. Merton teaches:

> The Christian solitary, in his life of prayer and silence, explores the existential depths and possibilities of his own life by entering into the mystery of Christ's prayer and temptation in the desert, Christ's nights alone on the mountain, Christ's agony in the garden, Christ's transfiguration and Ascension. This is a dramatic way of saying that the Christian solitary is left alone with God to fight out the

question of who he really is, to get rid of the impersonation, if any, that has followed him into the woods. He thus receives from God his "new name", his mysterious identity in Christ and His Church.[34]

The discovery of the presence of Christ within and the emergence of the true self in the solitude and silence of contemplation is, first of all, life. It is the realization of one's identity as a child of God in darkness, emptiness and poverty. An indication of the contemplative insight into the true self is found in a meditation written in the hermitage in the middle of the night.[35] Merton shares this insight:

> One might say I had decided to marry the silence of the forest. The sweet, dark warmth of the whole world will have to be my wife. Out of the heart of that dark warmth comes the secret that is heard only in silence, but it is at the root of all the secrets that are whispered by all the lovers in their beds all over the world. So perhaps I have an obligation to preserve the stillness, the silence, the poverty, the virginal point of pure nothingness which is at the center of all other loves. I attempt to cultivate this plant without comment in the middle of the night and water it with psalms and prophecies in silence.[36]

The realization of being rooted in the ground of existence in identification with the life of God and His creation simplifies the life of the solitary. The first hermit of Gethsemani demonstrates this simplicity:

> I exist under trees. I walk in the woods out of necessity . . . . What I wear is pants, what I do is live. How I pray is breathe.
> I am out of bed at two-fifteen in the morning, when the night is the darkest and most silent. Perhaps

this is due to some ailment or other. I find myself in the primordial lostness of night, solitude, forest, peace, a mind awake in the dark. A light appears, and in the light an ikon. There is now in the large darkness a small room of radiance with psalms in it. The psalms grow up silently by themselves without effort like plants in this light which is favorable to them. The plants hold themselves upon stems which have a single consistency, that of mercy, or rather great mercy. Magna misericordia. In the formlessness of night and silence a word that pronounces itself: Mercy . . . [37]

In revealing his life Merton does not mean to imply that the solitary is somehow better than others but that contemplatives, particularly hermits, are called out of the ordinary to explore areas which others will never enter. This exploration is necessary for a deep and fully valid human existence and a valuable religious development, for it is in the desolate region of solitude that the human person experiences aloneness with God. In fact, Merton articulates:

It is possible to stumble around and make a lot of mistakes . . . but the good Lord is always there and He helps us to learn more and more what his grace means because the solitary life is not a life of great powers and heroism but a life of direct dependence on grace and we realize more and more our own weakness and nothingness and foolishness . . . . [38]

Just as the life of the Christian solitary does not imply that one is somehow better than others, neither does it mean that the one alone has no relationships with the persons of the world, the Church or the monastery. Merton reiterates, "It is necessary that we find in the silence of God not only ourselves but also one another. Unless some other man speaks to us in words that spring from God and communicates with the silence of God in our souls, we remain isolated in our own silence, from which God tends to withdraw".[39] This silence is not that of the individual who has gone out into the desert to receive special messages denied to the many; this type of solitude is filled with the false self and results in separation because the one alone marks himself off from others. Genuine solitude is that which unifies, not divides; it is not a seeking of self but a loss of self. In listening to the ground of being the solitary identifies himself with all in universal love. In this solitude all persons are at once together and alone.

The hermit recognizes that solitude is a basic and inevitable human reality which is the foundation of a deep, pure and gentle sympathy with all others. Through that solitude the hermit enters into the mystery of God and brings others into that same mystery of love. Faithfulness to the solitary vocation is important for the world.

> If the solitary should one day find his way, by the grace and mercy of God, into a desert place in which he is not known, and if it is permitted to him by divine pity to live there, and to remain unknown, he may perhaps do more good to the human race by being a solitary than he could have done by remaining the prisoner of the society where he was living.[40]

The hermit's obligation to the world is to be true to God and his inner self, to be healed and transformed in the prayer of silence and solitude, and in the transcendence of self, to be united to God, self and others in love. This commitment also makes the solitary fully and perfectly a person of the Church.

The Christian solitary has a special function in the mystical body of Christ. This function, of which Merton writes, is paradoxical, because in living outwardly separated from the community, the hermit, whether conscious of it or not, is a

vocation of hermit

witness to the transcendental nature of our unity through Christ in the Holy Spirit. He explains:

> The hermit remains to put us on our guard against the natural obsession with the visible, social and communal forms of Christian life which tend at times to be inordinately active and become deeply involved in the life of secular non-Christian society. The average Christian is in the world but not of it. But in case he might be likely to forget this—or worse still in case he might never come to know it at all—there must be men who have completely renounced the world: men who are neither in the world nor of it . . . [41]

The Christian solitary may live closer to the heart of the Church than the one who struggles in the midst of apostolic activity. Even in hiddenness and insignificance the hermit lives as a prophetic witness to God's love for the human person in Christ, and to the Church's own charismatic heritage.

In addition to his relationship with the world and the Church, the Christian hermit, if he is to remain faithful, must be supported and understood by the monastic community to which he belongs. The hermit remains within the framework of monastic obedience and community, even when that implies a certain freedom from institutional structures. The community assists the solitary to remain faithful by their prayers and material aid, as well as by their love and understanding. In return the hermit "owes his solitude" to the community; his depth of prayer and awareness, as well as his faithfulness, are witnesses to the Kingdom of God. It is to his brothers in the monastery that Merton declares:

> The hermit remains . . . to prove, by his lack of practical utility and the apparent sterility of his vocation, that cenobitic monks themselves ought

to have little significance in the world, or indeed none at all. They are dead to the world, they should no longer cut a figure in it. And the world is dead to them. They are pilgrims in it, isolated witnesses of another kingdom. This of course is the price they pay for universal compassion, for a sympathy that reaches all.[42]

The relations of the hermit contemplative with persons of the world, the Church and the monastery are authentic, in so far as his relationship with God is the foundation of these relationships. This authenticity is a gift given in silence and solitude, in the dread and compunction of prayer, in the search for God and one's true self. The overwhelming importance of this search for Merton is emphasized by a friend who was his first official biographer:

All the private archival papers indicate one over-whelming fact: Tom was driven almost from the beginning to total abandonment to God: absolute and perfect. And in his struggles, the chief difficulty lay always in seeking to find ways to become more solitary, more united—seeking to remove the imperfections, the sounds and other things: he died really looking ardently for that place where there would be nothing but him and God in uninterrupted silence and solitude, far from the proximity of men, though united to mankind, but absent mankind.[43]

Solitude, silence, abandonment, poverty, purity of heart, humility, sitting in one's cell for the Name of God, compassion, true self and union with God are words used by Thomas Merton to express the reality of the solitary life. And yet his life of loving submission to the will of God remained largely unexpressed, hidden and secret in the most private of his relationships. Alone with God, longing to be submerged in His face and stripped of all to become the brother of Christ, Merton has and continues to share the fruitfulness of his solitude to reveal the Love of God.

Conclusion

The transforming journey of Thomas Merton is the dynamic story of a man within the milieu of the twentieth century, called by God to unity in love and the discovery of his true identity in Christ. This transformation was motivated and mediated by his continuous desire for greater solitude and silence, and expressed in terms of poverty, abandonment, mystery, faith and death in Christ. Merton grew in knowledge, experience and love to a greater understanding of the many facets of solitude both before and after he embraced the solitary life.

As a Christian hermit in the Roman Catholic Church and the Cistercian Order, Merton was influenced by biblical, patristic and monastic sources. From these he perceived the vocation of the hermit as a call into solitude and silence, a vocation in relationship with Christ in the Church. As such, it is a call from God, a response in love for God and an interior journey. Solitude, silence and love can be found in the ground of one's own being and it is in this ground that faith is actualized and one is enabled to responsibly accept transformation and transcendence. Such discovery and response necessitates an emptiness of soul, a spiritual poverty.

One facet of the spiritual poverty of which Merton speaks is the obligation of the solitary to sit in his cell for the Name of God. This Name becomes an interior spiritual cell in which God dwells and where the hermit becomes his true self. The poverty discovered within the spiritual cell may result in the acknowledgement of personal weakness, sorrow and insecurity. Here the hermit learns to depend directly on God without visible support and faces doubt which questions the very essence of existence. Here in contemplative prayer divine mercy transforms and elevates emptiness into perfect love and fullness.

The elements of the Christian eremetical life exist for the sake of living in loving union with God in Christ. This union is possible because the human person is created in the image and likeness of God. However, the failure to realize this fundamental orientation to God, effected by original sin, has disfigured the Divine Image within and the loss of likeness to God. The capacity for restoring likeness to God is made possible in the incarnation of the Logos.

It is in Christ that the human person is called to mystical union to be elevated, changed and transformed by grace. In transformation all are called as children of God in Christ, and in the discovery of the presence of God, the true self is revealed. The movement from the false self is the purifying search for Christ himself. The search in solitude is the life of the hermit, a life of simplicity, exploration and dependence, alone with God.

Although alone with God, the hermit is a prophetic witness to a solitude that is shared by everyone. Thus the hermit, although physically alone, remains in relationship with persons of the world, the Church and the monastic community, and through his faithfulness communicates the unity of the Trinity. Merton speaks of fidelity to the solitary life as he concludes:

> . . . the thing that sums it up for all of us (is) the great need for fidelity to God's grace, to understand the tremendous reality of the Cross and of grace and of love and of mercy in our lives. And to forget ourselves and surrender ourselves totally to the action of that grace which is beyond all understanding, and to praise Him in adoration and love and thanksgiving for the grace of Our Lord Jesus Christ and His Holy Spirit . . . .
>
> Let us realize that the Lord has called us to a very great and beautiful life, although it's completely hidden in Him—and that is really the beauty of it—to live this life hidden in Him, a life of complete rest in Him, complete . . . . [44]

Jean Leclercq

A COINCIDENCE
OF OPPOSITES

The privilege of old age means that for 55 years I have been a student and admirer of Maritain, and, for the last 18 years of his life—the decisive years—a friend and confidante of Merton. It is impossible to speak of people one has known and to whom one is indebted without a certain warmth.

In 1978, on the occasion of the tenth anniversary of his death, for which I was partly responsible since it was at my instigation that he came to Bangkok, I had various opportunities to speak about Merton in the light of the many letters he sent to me. At that time my interest focussed on points necessary to avoid certain misunderstandings of his personality, particularly with regard to the evolution of his monastic and eremitical vocation. My approach then was intimate and subjective. Here I would like to take a more objective point of view in order to consider his attitude toward truth. Naturally, this is inseparable from the journey of Merton the monk and the hermit, and also from his earlier secular evolution. He was not a philosopher, as he knew so well, but he had always been a thinker and an activist. It is on both these grounds that he had something in common with Maritain, and through these interests that he came to meet him.

As I knew Merton and Maritain, the common factors I noticed in both of them were: their contemplation overflowed into their social action and their sometimes radical commitment; both of them were marginal men, free from and for the world; they were continuously on the roads of the world, either physically (Merton more rarely than Maritain) or spiritually. In neither man was there any alienation from anything or anybody. On the contrary, they were constantly in communion with everything and everybody. In both Maritain and Merton, what struck me was the liberty and fidelity of their reconciliation of contemplation and commitment.

Maritain and Merton were obviously extremely different from one another. But both reached similar ways of life in the end. Merton put the matter in a letter to me dated November 18, 1966: "Jacques Maritain was here in October and we had a fine visit. He is very much a hermit now, and his latest book has added a hermit voice to the contemporary harmony (or disharmony). *Le Payson de la Garonne* is, I think, very fine".

This reference to the final stage in the evolution of Maritain and Merton is very revealing. What was common to Maritain and Merton was not the search for truth. They had the truth—the Truth—and they knew it. It was their quest to insert the truth into life which was common to them, not only into their private lives, but into the public life of their countries, of Christianity, of the Church, of the world. A similar observation could be made concerning other great men of that generation whom I knew and who knew Maritain as well, like two of my very dear masters and friends, Erik Peterson and Etienne Gilson. It was after entire life-times of striving to insert into life that Maritain ended up as a poor contemplative hermit, and that Merton died as a wandering "missionary" of monasticism.

The first memory I have of Maritain is a quotation of Rimbaud in *Art and Scholasticism* which I can still cite from memory:

Son cœur, plutôt contemplatif,
Pourtant saura l'œuvre des hommes.
(His heart, rather contemplative, nevertheless will appreciate the works of men.)

Contemplation and humanism—this was also the theme of Maritain's little book, *Religion and Culture,* which enchanted our youth as Benedictine novices of the mid-20th century. When we started studying philosophy, we used his first doctrinal basic books, *Cinq Leçons sur l'être,* for example. What helped us to make the synthesis between what later on I called *The Love of Learning and the Desire for God,* were these beautiful little books of Maritain the poet, the artist, the mystic. Behind the scene was always Raïssa, who in these years published a translation of the treatise of John of St Thomas on the gifts of the Holy Spirit. She rarely appeared in public with him, a fact which on one occasion provided the opportunity for a pleasant presentation (impossible to render into English) alluding to the Samaritan woman of the Gospel: *"Aujourd'hui, M. Maritain est venu sans sa Maritaine".*

As early as the mid-twenties Maritain the philosopher had to take a stand in the political arena in defending the Holy See after the condemnation of Action Française. *Pourquoi Rome a parlé* and his other writings on this affair were a great help to my generation in this time of deep confusion. In the thirties when I was a student in Rome I met and heard Maritain and Gilson who were the first two scholars (interestingly enough, for that time, both laymen) to receive honorary degrees from the new Angelicum restored under Pius XI by Fr Stanislas Gillet. In the meantime there had appeared the great synthesis of philosophy, theology and mysticism. *Les degrés du savoir.* This was the time when Fr Garrigou-Lagrange enjoyed his greatest prestige in the field of spirituality. He used to come to St Anselmo to give us talks. But Maritain added to this Thomist and Carmelite learning a flavor of literary art which made of his writings "things of beauty".

In the thirties when, after being at Rome, I was sent as a student to Paris, I attended the lectures of Gilson at the Collège de France. At the same time I followed everything that Maritain had to say to various audiences concerning contemporary Church and world problems. He was involved, but always a contemplative. One day I received an invitation to one of the philosophical tea parties that Raïssa and Jacques held in the mansion in Meudon. Printed in the corner of the card were the words, "On parlera des anges"—"Topic: Angels". This occurred at the time when Jews were being persecuted, first in Nazi Germany and then in Fascist Italy. Maritain, Peterson and my other master and friend, Father Anselm Stolz (who died prematurely in 1940), affirmed the mystery of the Jewish people as a witness of God. This shows Maritain never ceased to be a contemplative committed to human and religious interests.

Then came the war and his stay in the United States. I confess that after his return his delightful little book, *Reflections on America,* helped some of us to overcome the superiority complex that many Europeans felt towards the American way of life. He showed us that beneath the surface was a culture and a sense of humanity which were to develop richness in the decades to come.

I found the Maritains in Rome again when he was the Ambassador of France to the Holy See. In the meantime there had appeared a group of essays, dealing mainly with freedom and Christian humanism, which he had published in America and which were collected, first in French and very soon in English in such volumes as *The Range of Reason* (1952). All this gave Maritain the image of a liberal, even of a radical, and excited a certain opposition to him. In the late fifties when, with Christine Mohrman and a few others, we received honorary degrees from the Catholic University of Milan, Maritain had been on the list of the proposed candidates. But his name had been removed by the Sacred Congregation for Studies and Seminaries. When the story was told to a group of friends at a dinner in the French embassy to the Holy See, there was a unanimous protest which I can still recall: "We will write to Jacques to express our solidarity with him and our congratulations for his missed doctorate". But the day we recevied our diplomas, Archbishop Montini (recently made a cardinal by John XXIII) was there, and it was he who was to restore entirely the Roman reputation of Maritain.

These years of suffering and of retirement in solitude led him to his last articles in *Nova et Vetera* and his last books like *On Grace and on the Humanity of Jesus Christ,* in which he poured out his contemplation. To his knowledge of the traditional metaphysics of the Thomist and Carmelite traditions he had the courage to add new insights inspired by modern psychology which he developed in a personal way. Thus, for sixty years this man of God developed steadily, faithful to his first convictions enriching himself and his readers with all the resources of contemporary learning.

Philosophically and politically, Maritain had managed to remain free from every pressure, from one side or the other, and to remain free in his faith and in his thinking. He had been too free to receive certain forms of official recognition. I heard Gilson say: "I shall never enter the French Academy while Maritain is not a member". But he was never to be admitted, as Gilson realized later on. The message Maritain had delivered to us consistently had been one of reconciliation between the obedience of faith and the freedom to think, between a contemplative attitude and a disinterested involvement for justice and peace among men.

In comparing Merton and Maritain, as I cannot help doing, I see various fields of practical involvement in which they were in deep convergence, in spite of the very different circumstances in which they lived. At the basis of facing similar problems and as a prerequisite to any solution, I discern a common element: their spiritual culture.

We know from what Merton says in *The Sign of Jonas* that he was reading a great deal of Maritain, Gilson, and other great thinkers during his years of formation. He was not only gathering notions, learning facts and concepts, but also reflecting, judging, reacting personally, especially on a point which was central for Maritain and himself: the reconciliation of knowledge (theological and historical) and of personal spiritual experience. As an example, I shall quote a passage from one of the earliest of his letters which I have kept. It is of October 9, 1950. Commenting on some suggestions I had made in my book *Saint Bernard Mystique,* he writes:

> there is the evident desire of the saint to *penetrate* the text (of Scripture) with a certain mystical understanding and this means to arrive at a living contact with the Word hidden in the word. This would be tantamount to saying that for Bernard, both exegesis and theology found their fullest expression in a concrete mystical experience of God in his revelation. This positive hunger for "theology" in its very highest source would be expressed in such a text as Cant. lxxiii, 2: "Ego . . . in profundo sacri eloquii gremio *spiritum mihi scrutabor et vietam".* He is seeking "intellectum" and "Spiritus est qui vivificat: dat quippe intellectum. An non vita intellectus?"

Merton continues:

> As you have so rightly said (p. 488) "Sa lecture de l'E. Ste. prepare et occasionne son experience du divin". But I wonder if he did not think of Scripture as a kind of *cause* of that experience, in the same sense, servata proportione, as a sacrament is a cause of Grace? Scripture puts him in direct contact

with the Holy Spirit who infuses mystical grace, rather than awakening in his soul the awareness that the Holy Spirit has already infused a grace kindred to that spoken of in Scripture. Or am I wrong? In any case, words like "scrutabor" and "intellectus" tempt me to say (while agreeing in substance with all your conclusions) that there must have been a sense in which St Bernard looked upon himself both as an exegete and as a theologian in his exposition of the Canticle. Although I readily admit there can be no question of his attempting as a modern author might to "make the text clear" or to "explain its meaning". That hardly concerned him, as you have shown. But do you not think, that in giving the fruit of his own contacts with the Word through Scripture he was in a sense introducing his monks to a certain mystical "attitude" towards Scripture—not a method, but an "atmosphere" in which Scripture could become the meeting place of the soul and the Word, through the action of the Holy Spirit?

Perhaps these are useless subtleties: but you guess that I am simply exercising my own thought in order to confront it with the reaction of an expert and this will be of the greatest service to me in the work that has been planned for me by Providence. I am also very much interested in the question of St Bernard's attitude towards "learning", and feel that a distinction has not yet been sufficiently clearly made between his explicit reproofs of "scientia" in the sense of philosophia, and his implicit support of scientia in the sense of theologia, in his tracts on Grace, Baptism, and his attacks on Abelard, not to mention (with all due respect to your conclusions) his attitude to the Canticle which makes that commentary also "scientia" as well as "sapientia". Have you any particular lights on this distinction between

> science and wisdom in the Cistercians, or do you know of anything published in their regard? It seems to me to be an interesting point, especially to those of us who, like yourself and me, are monks engaged in a sort of "scientia" along with their contemplation! (It is very interesting in William of St Thierry.)

This abstract of a letter shows that Merton always thought about faith, contemplating its mysteries, and that he did so without drawing a dichotomy between knowledge and spiritual experience. For him—as much as for Maritain—the degrees of knowledge led from study, learning to mysticism. At the same time, he was concretely involved in a sort of monastic secularity: the physical activity of manual labor.

The first time I saw him, he was working in Gethsemani like any other monk. In a letter of August 21, 1953, he wrote: "We have had a busy summer with much harvesting and other farmwork. In addition to that, our cow barn burned down and we have also bought a new farm, so that everyone has been exceptionally busy and I am two months behind with practically all correspondence". But in the same letter he also denounced the danger of excessive material activity and defended his vocation to become a hermit: "One illusion which is very strong in this country still is the idea that the eremitical life is essentially 'dangerous' and 'impossible' etc. Some monks who claim to have a high contemplative ideal actually run down the solitary life, and show a preference for the rather intense activity which is inevitable in a big, busy monastery of cenobites. It is all very well to have a big, busy monastery; but why claim that this is the highest possible ideal of contemplation? The French have a good word for that: *Fumisterie*" ("mystification" or "practical joke".).

Thus, even within his own vocation, Merton was—and already in 1953—a protestor, a monastic radical, an activist involved in fighting for a less active type of contemplative life. In fact, the evolution which took place in the following years proved that his protest had been heard.

Merton's just-quoted statements echo this passage of Maritain:

> I believe that the spirit of contemplation is called upon to assume new forms, to make itself more pliable and bolder, to clothe itself in the love of one's neighbor in proportion as it spreads out into ordinary life. This means that action can be a disguise for mysticism, but it does not mean there can be a mysticism of action. There is no more mysticism of action than there is one of inertia. Stop now, says the Lord, wait a minute, keep quiet a little; be still and learn that I am God . . . Allow me to draw your attention to the fact that a book on the subject of contemplation written comparatively recently by a poet who became a Trappist sold tens of thousands of copies in the United States, as also the book by the same author in which he tells of his conversion. This is only the most trifling indication, but it interests me particularly because I have the highest regard for Thomas Merton, because for many years I have thought that the most active land in the world is obsessed with a latent desire for contemplation (*The Range of Reason,* NY, Scribners, 1961, p. 215).

A paper by Maritain which has been reprinted in *The Range of Reason* begins with this strong assertion:

> Whenever we have to deal with the ingredients of human history, we are prone to consider matters from the point of view of *action* or of the *ideas* which shape action. Yet it is necessary to consider them also—and primarily—from the point of view of existence. I mean that there is another, and more fundamental, order than that of social and political

165

> action: it is the order of communion in life, desire
> and suffering. In other words there must be recog-
> nized, as distinct from the category *to act for* or
> *to act with,* the category *to exist with* and *to suffer
> with* which concerns a more profound order of
> reality (*Ibid.,* p. 121).

This idea is developed magnificently in the body of this
chapter of *The Range of Reason. To exist with the people*
as the text says, is what the Little Brothers and Sisters of Jesus
do. It is understandable that Maritain ended his life with
them; he was consistent.

Merton always had the same sense of solidarity with the
poor, the weak and the oppressed. He did not think that it was
enough to pray for them or to do something for them. He
desired to exist with them. Consider the following passages
drawn from his letters: "May I ask your prayers in turn for a
new hope of mine—that perhaps some day we may make a
foundation in the Andes, and that I may be sent there if God
wills" (November 13, 1957). Two years later, speaking of his
desire to become a hermit in Latin America, he wrote (in his
only letter to me in French from which I attempt to translate
a few sentences):

> Obviously, I am who I am, and I always keep a
> writer's temperament. But I wouldn't go there to
> write and be known, but on the contrary to *disappear,*
> to find solitude, obscurity, poverty. Chiefly, to escape
> the collective falseness and injustice of the U.S.A.,
> which so much involve our monastery and the church
> in this country . . . It is possible that my health
> would not withstand the diseases prevalent in the
> tropics. In that case, I should renew my attempt else-
> where, perhaps in Europe, or in areas of the U.S.
> where there are Indians (November 19, 1959).

On July 18, 1967, he ended a letter with this invitation: "I hope you will come down here . . . I'd like you if possible to meet a woman theologian who has some strong ideas about monasticism having 'lost its soul' (she's a radical eschatologist and works with Negroes)". I had written to him from a monastery in Vietnam which had been partly destroyed in the Tet Offensive. On March 9, 1968, he wrote: "What you say of Thien An breaks my heart. I think of those poor monks, to whom I felt so close, and to whom I had written not so many months ago. I shall certainly pray for them very earnestly, especially in the Eucharist".

Witnessing to God, even unto the form of martyrdom, was an exigency of the Christian faith frequently mentioned by Maritain in the time when the Nazis were persecuting Jews and Christians. In the preface which he wrote for my book on Paolo Giustiniani, a Camaldolese hermit of the 16th century, Merton splendidly developed the theme of martyrdom as the highest form both of spiritual "annihilation" and of universal communion. He applied this to the solitary, and mystic, to St John of the Cross and to Giustiniani. Consider these phrases from the preface: "coincidence of humility and greatness in the experience of union", a "share in the humility and poverty of Christ", "solitude in his soul, in his all" and "universal love". Elsewhere he wrote: "And a life alone with God . . . reaches up to God himself, and in doing so, embraces the whole Church of God. Meanwhile the hermit supports this interior poverty of spirit with the greatest exterior poverty" (*Alone With God*, NY, Farrar Straus, 1961, Preface).

This sense of poverty, humility and solidarity led Merton to become a protestor on behalf of all victims of material power. He did what he could by praying, fasting and writing. In a letter dated November 11, 1965, he wrote: "Thanks for the clippings. The one on the non-violent fasting women was in part, a surprise. I did participate in a very mild way . . . Obviously, I did not go ten days without food, I'm not that ascetic. I took a week of ordinary lenten fast, as we have it here". But on

Jean Leclercq

other occasions, and increasingly so, he took a stronger stand. On March 9, 1968: "I have a very great problem about staying in America (U.S.A.) . . . Perhaps if this society is under judgement, I too should remain and sustain myself the judgement of everyone else . . . " No need to insist on these memories. Let it suffice to have suggested how deeply, how radically, this contemplative was involved in the problems of his time and his country.

A problem which Maritain faced courageously was, as the title of the eighth chapter of *The Range of Reason* has it, "The Meaning of Contemporary Atheism". What interpretation are we to give to the fact that in the modern history of the West, atheism has become so diffused? Has it answered the needs of so many people? Is this fact entirely negative? Does it not conceal some similarities, as well as enormous differences, between "the atheist and the saint"? This question has been the object of prolonged consideration. It appeared in a document in 1967, "The Message of the Contemplatives to the First Synod of Bishops", in which both Maritain and Merton showed a lively interest. Since then it has become a matter of current theological reflection.

In 1968 I asked Merton to give a presentation on Marxism and monasticism today at the forthcoming Pan Asian Monastic Conference in Bangkok. He immediately and enthusiastically answered:

> Thanks for your good letter about the arrangements for Bangkok. I will be glad to give the talk on Marxism and so on. Important indeed! I've familiarized myself pretty well with Herbert Marcuse whose ideas are so influential in the "students' revolts of the time. I must admit that I find him closer to monasticism than many theologians. Those who question the structures of contemporary society at least look to monks for a certain distance and critical perspective. Which alas is seldom found. The

vocation of the monks in the modern world, especially Marxist, is not survival but prophecy. We are all busy saving our skins.

The opposite of saving one's skin seems to be the acceptance of death. There are various kinds of death. The one Merton chose for himself, freely, when in good health and full activity was what he liked to call "to disappear". This was also to be the last word he said in public before he was electrocuted in Bangkok. The mystery of this voluntary disappearance was one he mentioned most frequently in his intimate letters, and not only during his last years. Already on August 11, 1955, he wrote:

> I realize that I have perhaps suffered more than I knew from this "writing career". Writing is very deep in my nature, and I cannot deceive myself that it will be very easy for me to do without it. At least I can get along without the public and without my reputation! Those are not essentially connected with the writing instinct. But the whole business tends to corrupt the purity of one's spirit of faith. It obscures the clarity of one's view of God and of divine things. It vitiates one's sense of spiritual reality, for as long as one imagines himself to be accomplishing something he tends to become rich in his own eyes. But we must be poor, and live by God alone—whether we write or whatever else we may do. The time has come for me to enter more deeply into that poverty.

A year later, in 1956, with a reminiscence of the *"todo y nada"* of John of the Cross about which Maritain had commented in *The Degrees of Knowledge,* showing the "practicality" of this high mystical teaching, Merton wrote:

The question of solitude is no longer any kind of a

question. I leave everything in the hands of God and find my solitude in his will, without being theatrical or glowingly pious about it. I am content. But the right kind of contentment is a perfect solitude. When one is more or less content with the "nothing" that is at hand, one finds in it everything. I do not mean "nothing" in a tragic, austere sense, but the plain nothing which is the something of everyday life. The life of a Benedictine does not require all the fierce strippings of a St John of the Cross, but the common way of life without exaltation (even in nothingness) is enough.

His most frequent words and images, when speaking of himself, are those which evoke obscurity, solitude and poverty: "I value your prayers in this time of my story and searching. It is more and more evident to me that someone must go through this kind of thing. By the mercy of God, I am one of those who must pass through the cloud and the sea. May I be one of those who reach the Promised Land" (January 3, 1955). Again:

The very idea of the solitary life is to live in direct dependence on God, and in constant awareness of our poverty and weakness . . . My chief reaction is a deep understanding of my poverty, and a feeling of solitude, which is a kind of lack of human support. True, one must go without support, one must learn to walk on water. But I like to think the Church is supporting me nevertheless, and that I am not merely wandering off on my own tangent (August 11, 1955).

This awareness of his own misery and this total trust in the Church really made Merton a committed contemplative: separated from all and united to all. It is through this reconciliation of poverty and solidarity, of solitude and communion, that he found peace and freedom for himself and was able to show the same to others.

Elena Malits

SOURCES AND SIGNS
OF SPIRITUAL GROWTH

Thomas Merton possessed a remarkable range of spiritual, intellectual, and imaginative gifts which found expression in the most diversified sorts of writing. He lived intensely and wrote compellingly out of his experience as a Christian contemplative, a monk-become-hermit, a man given to mystical prayer. He anguished deeply over the dehumanizing forces in contemporary society, and took on the prophetic task as a trenchant critic of violence and injustice. A passionate intellectual, Merton reveled in ideas and plunged into dialogue—at least through his journals—with theologians, philosophers, literati, artists, lively thinkers of every ilk. Merton was a prolific poet, a sometime-novelist, an inveterate essayist, a zany satirist, an astute literary critic, and a letter writer in the grand style. Not least, the Trappist monk was a serious and sympathetic student of the world's great religious traditions, especially those of the East. He wrote of them sensitively, attempting to discover

the authentic religious vision and values they embody, and
what Christians might learn from these traditions.

Thomas Merton was and did all these things. What ultimately will constitute his most important contribution remains
to be seen. In my estimation, however, Merton's greatest gift to
us lies in his autobiographical writing—including in that cate-
gory not only the youthful story which made him famous, but
also the several journals and many personal essays and poems
he produced right up to the end of his life. Almost all of Merton's writing might be described as having an autobiographical
dimension. In his articles on Zen, social issues, contemplation,
or what have you, he was engaged in communicating his own
consciousness of these realities and what difference they made
in his life. Merton was always involved in an open-ended
process of telling his own story. In a rather disjointed, but
nonetheless continuous, autobiographical narrative Merton articulated his ongoing quest for God, for his own identity, and for
the meaning of his life in relation to others. And Thomas
Merton would be able to express and position that elusive self-
development only as all autobiographical writers must: through
good metaphors for himself and his life in its various stages.

Any autobiographer is constrained to find the appropriate
metaphors which reveal the self enacting its story. The problem
is to discover the most expressive metaphors, ones which
illuminate the relationships between past, present, and possible
futures in a person's life. James Olney in his study of the
meaning of autobiography, *Metaphors of Self,* eloquently
describes the essential function of metaphor in this regard:

> A metaphor . . . through which we stamp our own
> image on the face of nature, allows us to connect the
> known of ourselves to the unknown of the world,
> and, making available new relational patterns, it
> simultaneously organizes the self into a new and
> richer entity; so that the old known self is joined to
> and transformed into the new, the heretofore un-

known, self. Metaphor says very little about what the world is, or is like, but a great deal about what I am, or am like, and about what I am becoming; and in the end it connects me more nearly with the deep reaches of myself than with an objective universe.[1]

As Roy Pascal puts it in his illuminating study, *Design and Truth in Autobiography,* "the purpose of true autobiography must be 'Selbstbesinnung', a search for one's inner understanding".[2] But there is no way to articulate a human being's "inner understanding" except through metaphors. A lifestory assumes its shape, moreover, by the convergence of metaphors which the autobiographical writer appropriates to suggest where he has been and where it is he now stands. Those same metaphors will also point to where he is going and to what the person might become.

If an autobiographical writer succeeds in discovering authentic metaphors for himself and the unfolding character of his life, they can reveal to him new possibilities for his own development. Good metaphors of the self serve as bearers of meaning to the writer who creates them. They disclose his present reality, but they also empower him to go on. We might say that an autobiographer's metaphors have a kind of "sacramental" quality. They function as signs indicating what is transpiring within the self. But, to speak analogously, they are effective signs: such metaphors enable the autobiographer to take hold of himself and to move in certain directions.

Thomas Merton, endemic poet and autobiographer he was, came up with many metaphors to suggest his self-understanding and the dynamism of his life. There is one which permeates his writing and provides a unifying scheme. Merton perceived himself as a man on a journey—the journey of ongoing transformation in the quest for God. The title he gave his early autobiography, *The Seven Storey Mountain,* captured Merton's view of his still-recently converted self and his call to the monastic life. Having been brought through hell, his vocation was to undergo a lifelong process of purification in search of the divine. And not long before he died in Asia, Merton announced the same theme in a circular letter to his friends: "Our real journey in life is interior: it is a matter of growth, deepening, and of an ever greater surrender to the creative action of love and grace in our hearts. Never was it more necessary for us to respond to that action".[3]

The metaphor of the journey, indeed, dominates and frames Thomas Merton's story. It is too comprehensive to deal with in this short paper. Rather, I would like to examine briefly two of Merton's metaphors for himself as a monk which characterize various stages of his development. These are related to the metaphor of Merton's life as a journey insofar as they represent particular points along the way. I would suggest that Merton's capacity to articulate where he was in a certain period through metaphors like these released in him the energy to pursue his monastic vocation with fresh insight and renewed vigor. One is tempted by several such metaphors: "the solitary explorer",[4] "a stranger",[5] "poor pilgrim".[6] I have chosen to consider, however, two which the autobiographer himself evidently considered sufficiently representative to use in titles for his published journals. Let us examine Thomas Merton as "Jonas" and as "a guilty bystander".

Merton's journal of the years between 1946 and 1952 was taken up with his dilemma in finding himself both a contemplative monk and a famous writer. He felt called to an ever deepening life of silence and solitude, yet was appointed to write by his religious superiors. While experiencing longing for inner stillness and undisturbed prayer, Merton was led by his own inner compulsions to ceaseless intellectual and literary activity. In this period when he was preparing for solemn vows, undergoing ordination, and beginning to assume responsibility in the monastery as Master of Scholastics, Merton named the self he encountered in his journal pages "Jonas". He was a reluctant prophet suffering from the burden of his gift, he must struggle with his conflicting desires and consent to his yet unknown destiny. Writing the prologue to the published version of the journal which he called *The Sign of Jonas,* the monk-writer said it this way:

> Like the prophet Jonas, whom God ordered to go to Nineveh, I found myself with an almost uncontrollable desire to go in the opposite direction. God pointed one way and all my "ideals" pointed in the other. It was when Jonas was traveling as fast as he could away from Nineveh, toward Tharsis, that he was thrown overboard, and swallowed by a whale who took him where God wanted him to go.
>
> . . .
>
> The sign Jesus promised to the generation that did not understand Him was the "sign of Jonas the prophet"—that is, the sign of His own resurrection . . . I feel that my own life is especially sealed with this great sign, which baptism and monastic profession and priestly ordination have burned into the roots of my being, because like Jonas himself I find myself traveling toward my destiny in the belly of a paradox.[7]

The metaphor of "Jonas" expressed precisely Merton's sense of himself during the latter part of his first decade in the monastery as one destined to live out his vocation with unresolved tensions. In *The Seven Storey Mountain* he had characterized the problem this way:

> There was this shadow, this double, this writer who had followed me into the cloister. He is still on my track. He rides my shoulders, sometimes like the old man of the sea. I cannot lose him. He still wears the name of Thomas Merton. Is it the name of an enemy?[8]

Identifying himself as "Jonas", however, enabled Merton to befriend the shadow-side of himself which could have destroyed his monastic vocation. That metaphor would offer no easy solution to the problems he experienced, but it did provide an imaginative pattern by which he could recognize the creative potential of his inner conflicts.

Knowing himself as "Jonas", Thomas Merton was more free to engage in the writing he always both wanted and did not want to do. The monk who ardently sought a life of pure contemplation was able to accept his writing propensities as a genuine spiritual discipline. "Jonas" articulated that insight poignantly:

> If I am to be a saint—and there is nothing else that I can think of desiring to be—it seems that I must get there by writing books in a Trappist monastery. If I am to be a saint, I have not only to be a monk, which is what all monks must do to become saints, but I must also put down on paper what I have become. It may sound simple, but it is not an easy vocation.
>
> To be as good a monk as I can, and to remain myself, and to write about it . . . [9]

Merton kept writing about it. And his understanding of what it meant for him to be a monk and to remain himself kept on developing. The journal published in 1965, covering material from notebooks since 1956, he entitled *Conjectures of a Guilty Bystander*. Here was a fresh metaphor for a Merton experiencing new demands and further growing pains. In this decade he had begun venturing beyond the monastery walls in his writings about social and political issues. Merton was, to be sure, concerned about the spiritual implications of war, racial strife, and the consumer society; nonetheless, a monk was moving on dangerous terrain in a world and a Church accustomed to separate all too neatly religious and secular topics.

It seemed a more sensitive, chastened Thomas Merton who

offered his readers in the mid-60s not apodictic statements, but simply "conjectures". He displayed the vulnerability of a man who consciously accepts his existence in an age of violent transition and cultural crisis. And he showed something of the liberating insight such acceptance might bring: "I do not have clear answers to current questions. I do have questions, and, as a matter of fact, I think a man is known better by his questions than by his answers".[10] The self Merton sought to know and share with others in this period was a probing self in an insecure and agonized society. It was a self-searching to work out the relationship of a contemplative monk to the world he described as marked by "desperation, cynicism, violence, conflict, self-contradiction, ambivalence, fear and hope, doubt and belief, creation and destructiveness, progress and regression, obsessive attachments to images, idols, slogans, programs that only dull the general anguish for a moment . . . ".[11] Merton called that monk's self facing that turbulent world "a guilty bystander".

It was a tensive metaphor, catching up all the ambiguities of Merton's situation and his grasp of what was being asked of him. "A confrontation of twentieth-century questions in the light of a monastic commitment", he averred, "inevitably makes one something of a 'bystander' ".[12] But was it the monk's posture on the sidelines of action needed to change the world which made him guilty? Not for Merton. Distance and true detachment from direct involvement could provide the contemplative's unique gift to society: critical perspective on its problems. Rather, what prompted Merton to announce himself guilty was recognizing his own real complicity in those problems. He had undergone transformation, yes; but it was insufficient and incomplete. As a "bystander" this monk was acknowledging that he had not yet spiritually grown so as to stand by the world in the way his vocation required. The metaphor of "guilty bystander" expressed a nuanced assessment. It articulated Merton's mature view of what had been accomplished in him and what yet remained to be done. Merton's own monastic world was, he said, "open to the life and experience of the greater, more troubled, and more vocal world beyond the cloister. Though I often differ strongly from that 'world' I think I can be said to respond to it. I do not delude myself that I am not still part of it".[13]

Understanding himself by means of this metaphor helped Merton to accept his common humanity as well as his special monastic call. It expressed his awareness of what he shared with everybody else. One "guilty bystander" described his street corner insight:

> In Louisville, at the corner of Fourth and Walnut, in the center of the shopping district, I was suddenly overwhelmed with the realization that I loved all those people, they were mine and I theirs, that we could not be alien to one another even though we were total strangers. It was like waking from a dream of separateness, of spurious self-isolation in a special world, the world of renunciation and supposed holiness . . . Not that I question the reality of my vocation, or of my monastic life: but the conception of "separation from the world" that we have in the monastery too easily presents itself as a complete illusion. . . .
>
> We [monks] are in the same world as everybody else, the world of the bomb, the world of race hatred, the world of technology, the world of mass media, big business, revolution, and all the rest. . . .
>
> This sense of liberation from an illusory difference was such a relief and such a joy to me that I almost laughed out loud . . . "Thank God, thank God that I *am* like other men, that I am only a man among others".[14]

The metaphor of "a guilty bystander" encapsulated Merton's grasp of the paradox of his life in the late 50s and early 60s the way "Jonas" had done it in the late 40s and early 50s. The monk-writer became the monk-prophet. "A guilty bystander" was not denouncing those sinners out there; he was addressing his unconverted self. He was calling himself to life—and now could insist that "the contemplative life is first of all *life,* and life implies openness, growth, development. To restrict the contemplative monk to one set of narrow horizons and esoteric concerns would be in fact to condemn him to spiritual and intellectual sterility".[15]

Thomas Merton's metaphors for himself certainly protected him from such sterility. He thought by means of them; he acted upon what they showed him. Unfortunately, since his last work of autobiographical writing was edited and published post-humously, we will never know what he would have called *The Asian Journal.* We can be sure Merton would have returned from his journey to the East with a new metaphor for where he had been, where he was, and where he would be going spiritually.

Mary L. Schneider

ECCLESIOLOGICAL
DEVELOPMENT

Thomas Merton was, above all, an ecclesial man. From his initial entry into the Catholic Church in 1938 through the formative and mature periods of his monastic life he remained deeply committed to the Church, a commitment which is everywhere reflected in his writings.

A close examination of these writings, particularly the autobiographical and those concerned with various aspects of monastic theology, reveals a process of development in Merton's understanding of both the nature and function of the Church. It is at once a development that is organic and consistent and a development that reveals a growing sophistication and maturity in his ability and desire to address the concrete problems and possibilities faced by a post-Vatican II community.

At its most basic and pre-conversion level, his understanding of the nature and function of "church" in a generic sense, is briefly alluded to in *The Seven Storey Mountain*. The young Merton, as early as the age of five, experienced a desire to go to church, a desire which recurred at various times throughout his childhood and teen-age years.[1] In retrospect he recognized in these desires the reflection of a universal, innate and natural human need to worship God as a creator. This coming together of individuals to acknowledge their common dependence on God both fulfilled a natural duty and satisfied a need.

> One came out of the church with a kind of comfortable and satisfied feeling that something had been done that needed to be done, and that was all I knew of it . . . . It is a law of man's nature, written into his very essence, . . . that he should want to stand together with other men in order to acknowledge their common dependence on God, their Father and Creator. In fact, this desire is much more fundamental than any purely physical necessity.[2]

But despite this sense of an "accomplished duty", Merton insisted that, for him at least, this natural desire was ultimately incapable of fulfillment through the various settings of Protestant worship to which he had been haphazardly introduced.

His critique of Protestant churches and worship was based on a retrospective post-conversion analysis and has to be understood in light of the sense of fulfillment he experienced in the more sacramental and liturgically-oriented Catholic tradition. Specifically, he recalled the attempt made by a French Protestant minister to impart some religious instruction to a then quite unreceptive and not quite teen-aged, Tom Merton. His assessment of that experience contained a denigration of what he considered to be a tradition which offered little more than "moralism" and an occasional vague sermon.[3]

His experience with the Anglican Church, during his early teens, proved to be somewhat better. Regular attendance at Sunday services drew out of young Tom a little "natural faith" which reflected in "many occasions of praying and lifting up my mind to God", a period of two years which he described as his "religious phase".[4]

But this, too, proved ultimately unsatisfying. He came to view the Anglican Church as one whose unity was based solely on social tradition. The sense of bonding was the result of a social cohesion, an alliance and identification with a particular British social class. His rather harsh reflections on the Church of England as "the cult of a special society and group, not even of a whole nation, but of the ruling minority in a nation", is perhaps explicable in part because of his own admitted acceptance of this ecclesial manner of living and valuing.[5]

But the major source and foundation of his criticism of Protestant churches, in general and of the particular ones in his experience, lay in his belief that they appealed to and indeed lived out of a natural order and that therefore, no matter how sincere and earnest the believers, those churches could not rise above the level of being based on pious speculation and sentiment and, as a social group, above the level of a natural gathering in which people gathered precisely as people, as neighbors, burdened with a self-conscious and human constraint in their worship.[6]

Later reflection on his belief experience with the Quakers in Douglaston, New York, revealed a further understanding of Protestant churches in relation to the Catholic: the Friends "are full of natural virtues and some of them are contemplatives in a natural sense of the word. Nor are they excluded from God's graces if He wills. For He loves them, and He will not withhold His light from good people anywhere. Yet I cannot see that they will ever be anything more than what they claim to be—a 'Society of Friends' ".[7]

This view included not only Protestant denominations but the non-Christian traditions as well. They all operated on a natural level. Even though he admitted his admiration for the Hindu monk Bramachari, he could still believe, in his *Seven Storey Mountain* period of the 1940s, that all Oriental mysticism could possibly be "reduced to techniques" and, if that were true, it was not mysticism at all but remained purely in the natural order.[8]

Nature and Function of the Church

In speaking of a "natural order", he was not denying that Protestant churches and non-Christian traditions could exhibit and indeed did have an earnest and pure worship of God. There existed, however, an ontological distinction between them and the Catholic church in that they could be the *recipients* of grace, but that the *origin* of that grace lay in the Catholic church as the *Body of Christ.* Thus the *source* of grace lay elsewhere than in those traditions.

This critical distinction for Merton was based on his experiential appropriation of an ecclesial model of the Catholic church understood as the Body of Christ. This distinction is what enabled him to differentiate between the "natural" association of Protestant denominations and what he considered to be a radically different foundational identity for the Catholic church, a foundational identity which allowed him to describe it in terms of its having a "supernatural" rather than a "natural" base/source of its existence and unity.

In his discussion of the nature and function of the Church, the term "Body of Christ", occurs again and again and emerges as the key concept upon which he develops an understanding and analysis of the ecclesial community.

This discussion can perhaps best be dealt with by dividing his overall thought into a number of distinct yet interrelated areas, the first of which can be considered his direct references and reiterations of the reality of the Church as being the Body of Christ. For him this establishes it as the "only true Church",[9] the one established by Christ himself.[10] As such, the Church lives in Christ and in the Spirit.[11]

Several corollaries follow from this. First of all, the Church becomes, then, an embodiment of the true understanding of what Christianity is.

What is Christianity but the mystery of Christ in us, the mystery of Christ in His Church, the mystery of our salvation and union with God in Christ Jesus?

. . .

This mystery is our incorporation in Christ. It is the holy and eternal design of God the Father to save us in Christ His Son, . . . to *re-establish all things in Christ,* that are in heaven and on earth, in Him". (Eph. 1)
The "re-establishment" of all things in Christ means the spiritualization of all creation through contact with the sacred humanity of the Word. The Man-God Jesus Christ reigns in heaven. But He is present and He acts on earth in the members of His Body, the Church. All who are incorporated in Christ by faith and baptism share with Him His divine sonship, and enter with Him into the mystery of His divine life and power.[12]

Secondly, the Church serves as the locus for the presence of Christ to and in the world, a sanctifying presence that is the source of grace through which the world is ultimately sanctified. "All grace reaches us in and through Christ as head of the Church".[13] For Merton, this presence was also the true source of the *unity* of the members and thus his assessment of the Anglican Church (which included the belief that the members were united only through a social bond) was based on the notion that grace was "wasted" in that tradition because of its "lack of vital contact with the Mystical Body of the true Church . . .".[14]

Thirdly, it is precisely this energizing presence of Christ which is being and has been continually concretized historically through the Church's sacramental activity, particularly the liturgy of the Mass in which "Christ Himself, by His Holy Spirit, prays and offers sacrifice in His Body, the Church".[15] It is in the Eucharist that Christ holds the world together and through the Eucharist that grace enters into the world, even to those who do not know or believe in Him.[16]

Sacramental activity (and especially the liturgy of the Mass), becomes, then, the saving activity of the Body through which grace is somehow present and offered to all. While Merton acknowledged that other religious activity, such as the sermons and prayers he was exposed to in France, could be a means of grace, they were, nonetheless, in comparison with sacramental activity, "practically useless".[17] The major difference was that the efficacy of sacramental activity did not at all depend on the spiritual vitality of the minister. The Catholic understanding of *ex opere operato* ensured the presence of the grace ritually-enacted in word and deed.[18]

The emphasis of Merton's on the importance of sacramental activity appears to have resulted most basically from his actual experience of it. He had previously, upon reading Huxley's *Ends and Means,* come to disparage Christianity as "less pure" because it was immersed in matter, i.e., it utilized material creation as a means to achieve spiritual ends.[19] In retrospect, he could even allow for the mediation of grace through the material and natural as he reflected on his own journey to the Church.

> All our salvation begins on the level of the common and natural and ordinary things . . . . And so it was with me. Books and ideas and poems and stories, pictures and music, buildings, cities, places, philosophies were to be the materials on which grace would work.[20]

But no matter what served as a means of grace, the source was always the presence of the risen Christ localized in his Body, the Church.

With this basic ecclesial model, Merton could move easily to defining and understanding his own role within the Body as monk and priest. The monk enters a monastery in order to deepen his union with the risen Christ, to immerse himself in the hidden life of the Body and to grow in his love and concern for the rest of the Body throughout the world.[21] All of the liturgical and private activity of the monastery serves as the monk's road to God. For example, the liturgical praise of the divine office is "the collective interior prayer of persons who are fully conscious of themselves as members of Christ".[22]

This membership, for Merton, bears with it a personal obligation that is a necessary correlative and corrective to a too-facile understanding of the concept of *ex opere operato*. While the doctrine of sacramental efficacy remains valid, there is a corresponding emphasis in his thought on the interiorization and personal appropriation of the attitudes and actions which should characterize one who has been incorporated into the Body of Christ. Therefore, liturgical prayer needs to be personal and interior. Otherwise, it is not even prayer at all for the individual monk. Thus in all he does, the monk needs to be mindful that he is seeking to discover Christ and to be found in Him and not simply fulfilling his monastic obligations.[23]

The role of the priest is most fully discussed in *The Sign of Jonas* and in the essays that comprise *The Monastic Journey*. The model for priesthood is Christ himself as high priest in the midst of his people. It is his prayer which is offered to the Father through the Spirit in all liturgical activity . . . . "Jesus the head of the Church is present with His whole mystical body, offering praise to the Father and sanctifying the souls of men".[24]

Merton's understanding of his own priesthood was marked with this strong sense of the unity of the Body. He felt a responsible link between his Masses and the spiritual welfare of all the members of the Body. Noting that his subdiaconate duties included "officially praising God for the Church and for the whole of creation",[25] and doing this as consistently as he could, he stressed the public and corporate nature of priesthood in the Church and also the link between his own priesthood and that of Christ as high priest.[26]

In fact, the two merge into a united yet distinguishable reality with the priest being revealed as an *alter Christus:*

> My soul is united to the soul of Christ in the priestly character impressed upon me and in the Mass His soul and my soul act together as closely and inseparably as two rays of light shining together.
>
> . . . it seems to me as if, without ceasing to be who I am, I had become Somebody else—as if I had been raised to a higher and much simpler and cleaner level of being.[27]

The experience of his priestly functioning and his understanding of the nature of his priesthood were strongly linked to the Church's own self-understanding in the 1940s and 1950s: the Church as the Body of Christ, the priesthood as an entering into the mystery of the sacrificial priesthood of Christ, present as victim and high priest in the midst of the Church. While Merton's exposure to ecclesiology included both a monastic theology and the traditional scholastic interpretation of the subject, it was, perhaps, the re-emphasis and renewal of the concept of the Church as the Body of Christ which influenced him most. *Mystici Corporis* (Pius XII, 1943) and *Mediator Dei* (Pius XII, 1947), provided the necessary contemporary framework of understanding for him. Indeed, it is to *Mediator Dei* that he refers most in his discussions of liturgy and priesthood[28] and no other term to describe the Church occurs more often than "Body of Christ" or "Mystical Body".

These documents provided him with the expressed ecclesiology of the Church at the crucial time of his immersion into the Catholic "experience" (liturgical, monastic) and the Catholic "traditions" (scholastic, patristic).[29] He interpreted his own experiences through this ecclesiology and it was to remain, I believe, the most viable understanding for him as he moved his thought into broader frameworks that encompassed the world, the ecumenical movement, and the traditions of the Far East.

The Church as Community/Institution

Most of the reflections on the relationship between church as community and church as institution, as Body and as organization, are found in *Conjectures of a Guilty Bystander,* which Merton describes as notes expressing his version of the world in the 1960s (although some material dates back to notebooks kept since 1956).

Previous to these, however, are several remarks which establish his attitude in the 1940s toward the institutional and hierarchical nature of the Church. *The Seven Storey Mountain* relates a pre-conversion hostility, fear and distrust of institutional Catholicism (the only understanding he had at that point) that was, in part, the result of his own grandfather's hostility. This view was left virtually unchallenged for years, ultimately affecting even his choice of reading material. As he recounts, he had a terrible sense of disgust and betrayal upon spying the "Imprimatur" in Gilson's *The Spirit of Medieval Philosophy* which marked its Catholic orthodoxy.[30]

This attitude was gradually supplanted by one which came to view the institutional church in a new light. The institution was seen to be the guarantor of the legitimate traditions and truths which Protestants had lost sight of through their severance from Rome. The Catholics had solid doctrine, a consistent, unified, continuous and vital tradition which was protected and maintained by the teaching magisterium and church authority.[31] Speaking "in the name of Christ as it were in His own Person",[32] the Pope, bishops, and those in authority performed the function of preserving and reiterating the revelation spoken of in tradition.

Although this function was never denied by Merton, he did move in the late 1950s and 1960s to a stronger delineation between the necessity of office in the Church and the need to continually reform its concrete self-understanding and function. The visible, institutional Church and its offices did not exist to serve itself nor to acquire more power in the world:

> . . . it is the Church's function to serve, to suffer, to preach, to witness on earth, and not to rule. Certainly she rules herself and makes laws to organize her own life, but only in function of her mission and her service to the world.[33]

The critical distinction which had to be maintained between the Church as Body and as institution had been overshadowed in the Post-Tridentine desire to defend the visible Church and strengthen its structure through increased legalism. In so doing, an equation had appeared between obedience and holiness so that "no distinction is made between Church as a community of persons united in love, and as an institution to which individuals are organized by law—so that their obedience to law becomes, in fact, an epiphany of the holiness of Christ".[34]

Vatican II was the end of the Counter-Reformation attitude which had diminished and overshadowed the ontological nature of the Church as Body and had confused it with the temporal and transient institutional structure. The gathering of *bishops,* Merton believed, would draw attention to the "diversity-in-unity of the universal Church which is not simply a corporation with a head office in Rome".[35]

This problem of imbalance and the need to rectify it through a renewed ecclesiology stemmed not only from Merton's experience of the Council and its movement beyond Trent, but also from a growing personal sense of independence from structures, born of his experiences of solitude, in which he could break free of the "exorbitant claims of society and of institutions"—a breaking free that encompassed Church legalism.[36] Thus he was free of the need to cling to the Church as "mere institution and womb" and could easily move into an exploration of the new relationship of Church and world which the Council had embraced.

The Church and the World

The relationship of Church and world can be divided (artificially, but, I believe, validly) into a discussion that includes, first of all, Merton's personal feelings toward the world, secondly, his views on the relationship of Church and world and, lastly, his understanding of the world as the arena for the Church's social concern.

Much of *The Seven Storey Mountain* conveys an attitude of distrust and dismay at the sinfulness of the world and the pervasive presence of evil within social structures. While this has to be understood in light of his post-conversion feelings regarding his own life and conduct as well as his assessment of the overwhelming political and social problems of the 1940s, there is never a complete break with the world and its problems nor a complete rejection of the world as totally and irretrievably evil.

As his monastic experience deepened and as he grew in his understanding of the Church as Body of Christ with its emphasis on the relatedness and mutual responsibility of the members, one to another, it is not surprising that he began to stress his relationship to the world from a different perspective. While still evil in much of its orientation, he could admit that he existed in solidarity with all men and shared their sinfulness and their need for redemption.[37] Addressing the problem of "the world" in relation to the contemplative life, he noted that the monk is called to compassion for the world, an openness which meant "being aware of and responsive to the real situation of people in the world, the critical problems of the world . . . . Simple aloofness, withdrawal, and refusal of concern would make the contemplative a scandal to his brother".[38]

This warning to contemplatives held true for the Church as a whole and especially for its visible, institutional element. Merton's assessment of the Church's relationship to the world prior to Vatican II was that it had abused its identification as Body of Christ through a process of rationalization to certain consequences which demonstrated a contempt for the world, a contempt which was, then and now, totally inappropriate.

The Church had adopted a "Carolingian suggestion",[39] a world-view resulting from its acceptance into the political and cultural structures of the world, beginning with Constantine. This view refused to take the reality of the world seriously, focusing instead on its sinfulness and evil and on the task of the Church to redeem as much as possible of the situation as the ultimate and eternal guarantor of order and grace through the creation of "Christendom". This task, undertaken in terms of both a spiritual and temporal authority, tended to deny or at least overlook any positive, natural values inherent in the world.

> In the Carolingian world view it somehow happened that the idea of the world as an object of choice tended to be frozen. The "world" was identified simply with the sinful, the perilous, the unpredictable (therefore in many cases the new, and even worse the free), and this was what one automatically rejected . . . . The world was what one therefore did not choose.
>
> . . .
>
> . . . Christian society ("Christendom") conceived of itself as a world-denying society in the midst of the world. A pilgrim society on the way to another world.[40]

This *contemptus mundi* became, in time a mere formality of withdrawal for a Church which became, in its own involvement with the construction of a Christian "empire", ever more worldly in its own unique manner—seeking the same ends as the world, but with a different set of motives so that what was condemned was "not the 'world' as such, but a rival structure or simply 'our competitor'. Contempt for the world became not contempt for the objectives of the world but competition with the world on its own ground and for the same power, with contempt for its motives".[41]

In these situations, Merton saw several dangers. First of all, the Church had failed to distinguish between "the world" and "the flesh", with the latter being the correct object of ecclesiastical negative pronouncements.

Secondly, the acquisition of secular power not only denied the reality of the Church's mission and witness as Body,[42] but placed the Church in an inevitable position of hostility toward the world. This hostility had broadened into an all-encompassing defensiveness as the "world" began more and more to ignore and reject a Church it felt was no longer relevant or needed. Thus the initial and fundamental goal of service to the world became transformed into a struggle to preserve a diminishing power and influence.[43]

The proper attitude of the Church toward the world should be one of charity and forgiveness, an attitude which flows from the deepest identity of the Church as Body and which is manifested in service, suffering, preaching and witnessing.[44] Instead of "the place where men gather to decree that others are guilty and they themselves are innocent", the Church's task is to take upon herself the sinfulness of the world. The Church at once confesses the sins of all men as her own, and receives in herself the mercy that is offered to all men".[45] Only in this does the Church manifest her own holiness as the locus for the justice and mercy of God in Christ.

> The Church is holy because of the mercy of God that is in her, and not merely because of the absence of of sins. This mercy, the dynamic action of the Spirit of Love constantly going to and fro and healing the wounds of sin by forgiveness, must obviously be exercised in the midst of weaknesses and sins. The true freedom of the sons of God [i.e., the members] is therefore a freedom from preoccupation and fear, a freedom from resentments and hostilities, a freedom from pride and contempt . . . a freedom which . . . gladly takes upon itself the burden and

> the responsibility for the sins of the world, *destroying them by charity, and, wherever occasion presents itself, by forgiveness.*[46]

Merton envisioned a Church which far from being a triumphal, judgmental Church, implicated and indeed immersed itself in the sinful world through an openness of charity and forgiveness that reaffirmed the dual reality of its own identity: weak and sinful and yet also the locus for the justifying mercy of God.

He was, however, quick to point out that an openness to the world did not mean an uncritical acceptance of its values and orientations. Such an adaptation simply for the sake of survival was symptomatic of an underlying fear of losing "relevance" and was a basic denial of the Church's true nature.[47] It was "servitudes to certain standards of value" which Merton believed he had left behind in entering the monastery and the Church itself would do well to avoid a facile acceptance of these in the name of modernity or a misunderstood *aggiornamento.* Nevertheless, despite the possible pitfalls, the Church needed to acquire a healthy respect for the modern world and to be willing to enter into a mutual dialogue for the benefit of both or it would ultimately have no place in the world at all.[48] Of that he was convinced.

In fact, he viewed the true basis for Christian mission to the world as grounded in the fact that the Christian is "not of this world", but is freed by his faith from the myths and illusions, the psychic determinisms and obsessions of society. He is, then, called upon to preach a Christian independence of society's claims and arrogant demands.[49]

> The point then is not to convince "the world", in this sense, that it needs a Christian God . . . . What is important is to show those who *want to be free* where freedom really lies.[50]

The "Church has, as her first function of all, to disturb man and unsettle him . . . by challenging him to return to himself". In this she should be the "one hope of alienated man recovering himself and his freedom".[51]

Merton's growing concern and articulation in the 1960s for some of the most crucial enslavements of society—war, nuclear arms, racism, intellectual and personal oppression—drew him into a more critical assessment of the Church's role in society. And it was to the Church's own documents that he turned to find the basis for a renewed social policy and stance.

Most pertinent for him were Pope John XXIII's *Pacem in Terris* (1963) and the Vatican II *Constitution on the Church in the Modern World* (1965). Despite the fact that he also utilized other sources in clarifying his understanding and developing the ramifications, he nonetheless had an affinity for social encyclicals and for Vatican II constitutions and declarations. His first encounter with such works as *Rerum Novarum* (Leo XIII, 1891) and *Quadrogesimo Anno* (Pius XI, 1931) had perhaps come through his contact with the Catholic Worker Movement and the work of Baroness Catherine de Hueck Doherty in the early 1940s, and in *The Seven Storey Mountain* he had noted how few Catholics seemed aware of these social teachings.[52]

Not only were most Catholics unaware and uninformed about the social teachings, but the very structures of the institutional Church prevented her from "enfleshing" her own policies in any vital manner. While committed to social justice and human dignity and liberation, the Church was often equally committed to the social *status quo*. And very often pronouncements on specific evils were too cautious and too late, giving the correct impression of being a reactionary rather than a creative involvement.[53]

It is unfortunately true that the Church has to repent of remaining enclosed in parochial concerns, and turn to the outside world. To turn to the world is to recognize our mission and service to man and man's world. We are not in the world for ourselves, for our own spiritual advantage, but for Christ and for the world. We have a mission to reconcile the world with Christ. How can we do this if we do not "turn to the world"? At the same time, in turning to our fellow-man and loving him, we will ourselves be reconciled with Christ. What other point has there ever been in preaching the Gospel?[54]

This "turning to the world" involved an acceptance of the *"historical task of the Mystical Body of Christ* for the redemption of man and his world".[55] The Church need only re-emphasize courageously its own primary nature which includes the constitutive element of being present in and related to the world and its problems in a dialectical and dialogical manner—a manner in which the Gospel is preached and incarnated as a radical and continual challenge to mankind, focusing on both the concrete situations in need of redemption and on the broader, more pervasive illnesses of mass society.[56]

In confronting both the concrete situations and the pervasive currents of dehumanization, Merton noted that what was at stake was the continued existence of civilization itself. "In the words of Pope John XXIII in *Mater et Magistra* [1961]: 'Today the Church is confronted with *the immense task of giving a human and Christian note to modern civilization:* a note that is almost asked by that civilization itself for its further development *and even for its continued existence'* ".[57]

But "modern civilization" here was not synonymous with Western civilization; the term extended to include the entire globe. If previously the Church had identified with and concerned herself with Western culture primarily, this was not to be so in the future. Referring to a 1955 letter of Pius XII, Merton pointed to the need for the universality of the Church to be manifested in concrete policies regarding the pluralism of cultures: " 'The Catholic Church is not one with western culture; she never identifies herself with any one culture, and she is ready to make a covenant with every culture. She readily recognizes in every culture what is not contrary to the work of the Creator' (letter of June 27, 1955, to the Bishop of Augsburg)".[58]

In this recognition of pluralism the Vatican Council II's strong affirmation of the dignity of the human person would be concretized not only in the assertion of the inalienable rights of the individual, but also in the assertion of the legitimate rights of human societies and cultures. This would, in turn, reinforce the reality of the Church as being "in" but not "of" the world, accepting the vocation of suffering, serving, witnessing, and would preserve her from any temptations to repeat the attitudes and actions associated with the "Carolingian suggestion".

The Church and Ecumenism

While Merton's understanding of the relationship of the Church to the world had grown, so had his understanding of the relationship of the Church to both Christian and non-Christian traditions. The sense of having deepened and experienced the depth of Catholicism had influenced his early judgment of other traditions, a judgment that he would later revise. Although he had allowed for the possibility of grace present in all traditions, he had been, nonetheless, convinced that they operated from a "natural" base and not from the "supernatural" foundational identity of the Church. Not only did he, in *The Seven Storey Mountain*, disparage his own pre-conversion attitude that "every religion was good; they all lead to God, only in different ways, and every man should go according to his conscience, and settle things according to his own private way of looking at things",[59] but he had gone so far as to claim that it was probably contact with the Fathers of the Church which was responsible for the holiness he encountered in one of his Protestant acquaintances, a holiness he was sure was not often found among Protestants.[60]

Without apologizing for the positions he had articulated in the autobiography, he did acknowledge that he had passed beyond them—in a growth of perspective that had, to a great extent, paralleled the Church's own development.

And so, in light of Vatican II, the Church's movement of turning to the world, to Christians and to non-Christians, was given ready acceptance by Merton who had, in fact, already been prepared for such a shift from parochial concerns and attitudes by his wide interests, his reading and his varied acquaintances. And he was prepared to make a contribution to the Church's own entry into such a journey with the Vatican II redefinition of the Church as the People of God, a pilgrim people.

This new statement of the reality of the Church served to reiterate and emphasize the belief that the Church had to approach the rest of the world with the seriousness and the attitudes that ought to mark her identity as Body. While still accepting the validity of the concept of Body, the idea of a "pilgrim people" served to underscore the Church's commitment not only to manifest the presence of Christ, but to search out and recognize it also in the experiences and expressions of others. It also served to underscore the transciency of the institutional element of the Church—a pilgrim people who cannot become frozen into organizational forms which both stifle the spirit and narrow the horizons and possibilities for the discovery of the spirit in others.

Merton accepted these ramifications of the new understanding of the Church and symbolized them in his own growth of openness. Through liturgy and community, through study and solitude, through prayer and searching, he came himself to the experience spoken of by Vatican II that . . . "while we are rediscovering the meaning of oneness as the People of God, we are also becoming aware of the fact that we are a pilgrim community traveling in the wilderness under the guidance of God ...".[61] Merton was an ecclesial man in all aspects.

Gordon C. Zahn

THE SPIRITUALITY
OF PEACE

The term, "prophet", is used freely these days, perhaps too freely, but we need not be hesitant about applying it to Thomas Merton. Nowhere is it more justified than in matters bearing upon Christian responsibilities with respect to war and peace. In published writings and personal communications Merton was a prophet in every sense of the term.

Like the prophets of the Old Testament he recognized the true dimensions of the corruption and evil of his time and tried to speak the saving word—sometimes in scathing denunciation of specific acts and prevailing trends; more often in inspirational exhortations calling Christians to a fuller and purer testimony to the faith they professed and a more effective performance of their personal responsibility to continue Christ's ministry of peace. If the call was ignored and those in power less responsive than the oppressor of past ages, the fault was not his. In true prophetic style he struggled on, making of his monastic cell (and later his hermitage) a center of spiritual resistance to an immoral war then in progress and, no less crucial, to the war that lies ahead, a threat to the future existence of our planet and all the creatures which inhabit it.

In this he had the prophet's gift of foresight. True, his works record no extraordinary visions or supernatural revelations. Instead, the foresight lay in his uncanny ability to see distant consequences, spiritual as well as historical, in the policies and practices of the moment. For instance, in dealing with a relatively short-lived controversy over a theologian's proposition, published in a popular Catholic journal, that a householder would be justified in shooting a less provident neighbor who tried to intrude upon the family backyard fall-out shelter, Merton saw the underlying truth that was not faced then—and one only vaguely grasped by the American bishops in their pastoral letter, "The Challenge of Peace: God's Promise and Our Response". He concludes his brief commentary:

> . . . Let us for the love of heaven wake up to the fact that our own minds are just as filled with dangerous power today as the nuclear bombs themselves. And let us be very careful how we unleash the pent-up forces in the minds of others. The hour is extremely grave. The guarded statements of moral theologians are a small matter compared to the constant deluge of irresponsible opinions, criminal half-truths and murderous images disseminated by the mass media. *This problem is going to be solved in our thoughts, in our spirit,* or not at all. It is because the minds of men have become what they have become that the world is poised on the brink of total disaster (*Nonviolent Alternative,* p. 105).

Merton was not around—at least not in the flesh—to contribute the insights of his prophetic wisdom to the work of the Bernardin Committee, yet many of his observations in published articles and his unpublished "Cold War Letters" find echoes in the pastoral's text. The bishops' telling image of "a new moment" which moved them to undertake a full moral analysis of nuclear war and its implications for the Church (and for all humanity) was an image familiar to this cloistered Trappist. Today what some may have dismissed in the 1960s as too apocalyptic a view of where the world was headed is at best a faint approximation of the threat we face. Jonathan Schell's recent book, *The Fate of the Earth,* deserves the attention and praise it received, but Merton was writing on that theme decades before. And what Schell protests as an "alliance with death" is put into even starker terms in Merton's warning that what is really involved is nothing less than the "free choice of global suicide", a "moral evil second only to the Crucifixion".

Schell concludes his book on the hopeful note that we may yet avoid sinking into "the final coma" by awakening to the truth of our peril in time to "break through the layers of our denials, put aside our fainthearted excuses, and rise up to cleanse the earth of nuclear weapons". He does not tell us what will bring about this saving awakening, however. Merton, too, offers hope, but he expresses it in more contingent terms: "The most urgent necessity of our time is therefore not merely to prevent the destruction of the human race by nuclear war . . . It must be possible for every free man to refuse his consent and deny his cooperation to this greatest of crimes" (p. 214).

There is yet another sense in which Merton deserves honor as a prophet. His influence continues and expands in the ever-escalating body of literature inspired by him and his works. And this is found not only in published articles, books, dissertations, etc. One of the sources I used in preparing this paper is the Harvard honors thesis written by a young colleague of mine at the Pax Christi Center on the topic, "Contemporary Catholic Theories of Non-violence". This young man [John Leary] of almost unlimited promise died at the age of 24, but in the few brief years of his activity in Boston's justice and peace community, he was deeply impressed as much by the intense spirituality of Merton's works as by their content. Dan Berrigan's tribute to this young man (". . . if Dorothy Day had had a son according to her wish, he would have been in the image of John") could apply just as well to Merton. It is comforting to know that there are other intellectual and spiritual "sons" of Thomas Merton keeping his influence alive in this time of desperate need.

A prophet, yes—but a pacifist too? The question must be raised if only because I will be discussing the spirituality of peace from a frankly pacifist perspective and borrowing heavily from Merton to support much of what I have to say. Merton's answer—at least as it is given in several of his articles—is in the negative. He was concerned about the tendency of pacifism "to take on the air of a quasi-religion as though it were a kind of faith in its own right" and the inability of the pacifist "to countenance any form of war since for him to accept any war in theory or in practice would be for him to deny his faith". As he saw it, "A Christian pacifist then becomes one who compounds this ambiguity by insisting, or at least implying, that pacifism is an integral part of Christianity, with the evident conclusion that Christians who are not pacifists have, by that fact apostatized from Christianity" (p. 33).

He is correct in everything he says—up to that howler of a nonsequitor at the end. It would take a gross display of spiritual elitism and pride (to which, I confess, some pacifists are prone) to ignore the fact that pacifism is still not accepted by the majority of today's Christians or to attribute that disagreeable fact to pandemic apostasy. Most pacifists I know (and this certainly is true of myself) do not fall into that tempting trap. They are more likely to follow the example of Franz Jaegerstaetter, the martyred Austrian peasant so admired by Merton, who when asked to explain why he stood alone in his refusal to serve in Hitler's army replied that his fellow Christians, including his bishop, had not been "given the grace" to see the immorality such service would represent.

Perhaps even such a claim to a special grace of insight might strike one as too condescending. All the pacifist says of those who do not see things his way and accept orders to go to war is that they are wrong (though not necessarily culpably wrong); or, if they do recognize the departure from Christian truth in the orders to kill and destroy and still persist in their obedience, an unfortunate weakness of will. This still sounds judgmental, and probably is, but it makes allowance, with regret, for the person who in perfectly good (however erroneous) conscience accepts war and service in war.

Again, was Merton pacifist? My answer is that, based on his writings and their analysis of how we came to be what we are and what it will take to change, he was more a pacifist than he was ready to admit—perhaps more than he was aware. There are points at which our positions differ, but they are few and not of major consequence. In its essentials my view of the spirituality of peace and its expression in protest and prayer finds support and validation in Merton's work. In some respects, it finds its origin there as well.

It is because of this support and validation that I presume to address the subject not only from the pacifist perspective but from that of the professional sociologist as well. This may seem to be a kind of scholarly heresy since sociology, as many practitioners of the discipline would insist, can have little to offer in so non-empirical a realm as the innermost structures of an individual's religious commitment. Merton, of course, would have his own objections having once gone so far as to thank God that he was not a sociologist!

He was wrong there too. Whatever else "spirituality" may mean and however much it is formed and sustained by the indefinable and immeasurable quality of divine grace, as a motive force in the individual's behavior it takes effect and operates through that individual's perceptions. The content and behavioral implications of such perceptions make it a proper subject of study in the sociology of perception.

To treat spirituality as a complex of motivating perceptions is not to reduce it to the level of the mundane. On the contrary, it contributes to a deeper understanding of the ways in which internalized values find expression in external acts and behavior. Does this mean that since every individual's perceptions must be his, or hers, alone that each person's "spirituality" becomes *ad hoc* and, in a sense, *sui generis?* Yes—and no. This would be true were it not for the processes of socialization which, even as they mold each of us into the unique persons we become, provide us with patterned similarities as well. From infancy on our development is guided, sometimes determined, through exposure to the same institutions (especially family, school, and church) and less structured, though still culturally conditioned, life experiences. Each individual and each individual's spirituality are "unique", but that uniqueness is better understood in most cases as a variation on a theme.

The principal components of the spirituality of peace are the perception one has of God; the perception of the proper relationship between believer and God (extending to the proper relationship of believer to believer); and the perception of the ultimate purpose and goal of those relationships. I would go so far as to suggest that any conceptualization of spirituality would have to begin with these.

Nor is there anything particularly different in the basic perception the pacifist has of God as all-powerful, all-knowing and, most important of all, infinitely loving and forgiving. His is the power to judge and to punish those who reject Him and His way to choose the path of evil, just as He promises eternal rewards to those who fulfill His will.

Pretty standard stuff to this point, one would agree. Nor do pacifists differ from their fellow Christians in their belief that this God became incarnate in the One whose followers we profess to be as a means of redeeming and saving His human creations. Unlike Homer's jealous divinities on Mt Olympus toying with their human pawns as it might suit their passing moods or fancy, the God of the Christian has more respect and infinitely more exalted plans for us. As Merton put it, this God "has chosen for Himself, in the Mystical Body of Christ, an elect people, regenerated by the Blood of the Savior and committed by their baptismal promise to wage war with the great enemy of peace and salvation".

At this point, though, we do encounter a point of crucial difference. The God of the *pacifist* Christian, because He has such respect and plans, would never seek to prove a point or display even righteous anger by condemning millions of innocent men, women and children to the dread scourge of war—and it certainly would not be His intent that those who claim to be His followers become the instruments of destruction and mass slaughter. Instead (Merton again), "He brought to His disciples a vocation and a task, to struggle in the world of violence to establish His peace not only in their own hearts but in society itself" (p. 13).

That wars come about through human fault and weakness cannot be denied, nor can we ignore the suffering and oppression they bring. But to attribute them to the punitive excesses of an angered Lord of Righteousness is to miss the point completely. The Christian is called to confront these evils in a spirit of sincere remorse, coupled with a firm attitude of complete confidence in—indeed, *abandonment to*—the saving goodness of God's will. In this we have moved to the consideration of that second basic perception, the relationship between God and believer. This is not to be mistaken for a fatalistic resignation to "what will be" but, instead, an active acceptance of that vocation and whatever it may require of one. Merton's "Prayer of Abandonment" expresses this beautifully:

> My Lord God
> I have no idea where I am going.
> I cannot see the road ahead of me
> and I do not know for certain where it will end.
> Nor do I know myself,
> and the fact that I think I am following your will
> does not mean that I am actually doing so.
> But I believe

that the desire to please you
does in fact please you.
And I hope
that I have that desire in all that I am doing.
I hope I will never do anything apart from that desire.
And I know that if I do this
you will lead me by the right road,
though I may know nothing about it.
Therefore will I trust you always.
Though I may seem to be lost and in the shadow of death,
I will not fear,
for you are ever with me,
and will never leave me
to face my perils alone.

Since we are all members of the same Mystical Body, this special quality of the relationship with God should carry over to our relationships with one another as well. "If we are disciples of Christ", Merton writes, "we are necessarily our brother's keeper . . . We cannot give an irresponsible and unchristian consent to the demonic use of power for the destruction of a whole nation, a whole continent, or possibly even the whole human race".

No better statement of the spirituality of peace as it bears upon our relationships with others can be found than the familiar peace prayer of St Francis. One pleads to be made an instrument of peace, to learn to replace hatred with love, injury with pardon, despair with hope—and so on. That term "instrument" must be understood properly, however. It does not imply a self-abnegating depersonalization making one a "tool" in the mechanistic sense; rather, it calls for a fully reasoned and freely willed surrender of self in total commitment—in that spirit of total, yet confident, abandonment so movingly expressed in Merton's prayer.

This is the "other side" of the pacifist's perception of God, and from it we derive the pacifist alternative to war and preparation for war, the theory and practice of nonviolence. We are told, and as Christians we presumably accept, that God's power is made perfect and manifest in our human infirmity; that no matter how perilous our situation may be, the gates of hell will not prevail. Of course this is no guarantee of "victory" or "success" as the world may define them; history provides evidence enough that those who appear to be the "good guys" are all too often victimized by the bad. But the same uncertainty of outcome is present in war—with the crucial difference that in war there is the certainty that people, all too often *innocent* people, will be hurt and killed. Now, given the nature of modern weaponry and the stated intent of national leaders to use them, the future existence of the planet is placed in doubt. One often hears the false charge that pacifists are indifferent to evil and the need to combat it. The commitment to nonviolence as an alternative to war is not indifference but, rather, a refusal to succumb to the delusion that it is somehow possible to overcome evil by adding to it.

Merton is too widely recognized as one of the leading apostles of Christian nonviolence to need citation on this point. His writings on the subject are so extensive and compelling that I do not hesitate to repeat what I have said elsewhere, that this will prove to be his major and most enduring contribution. As such they stand alone in their own right, but they also provide the transition to the third of the basic components mentioned above, the pacifist's perception of the ultimate purpose and goal to which we, as Christians are committed. In his "Footnote to Ulysses" he distinguished between nonviolence as the pursuit of truth (the nonviolence of the strong which can never fail) and nonviolence as a means to power (the nonviolence of the weak which carries no similar promise of success). It is surprising to find this admirer of Martin Luther King and ardent supporter of the civil rights movement (even, at times, its more radical Black Power variant!) striking a note which seems to distance himself from both. He writes of nonviolence, "It does not say 'We shall overcome' so much as 'This is the day of the Lord, and whatever may happen to us, *He* shall overcome' " (p. 75). It is here, in the eschatological dimension of nonviolent resistance that Merton makes his most significant contribution to the spirituality of peace.

His frequent use of the term, "post-Christian era" takes on a double meaning in the context of nonviolence. Most obvious, of course, is the lesson that Christians can no longer act (assuming they ever could!) in the confidence that secular authorities will take Christian principles into account in formulating their programs and policies, especially those related to international relations and conflict. The long history of warfare does not provide many—one might suggest *no*—instances of rulers or generals incorporating the limits imposed by the conditions of the "just war" so carefully elaborated by St Thomas and others into their strategic planning or military operations. However fervently the rhetoric of war might continue to extol religious themes and virtues, one cannot ignore the fact that the missiles launched from even a "blessed" Trident submarine (that "Auschwitz of Puget Sound" as Archbishop Hunthausen named it) were designed and are intended to commit precisely those "offences against God and man himself" condemned by Vatican II.

It is as Merton said: "We are no longer living in a Christian world . . . Today, a non-Christian world still retains a few vestiges of Christian morality, a few formulas and cliches, which serve on appropriate occasions to adorn indignant editorials and speeches. But otherwise we witness deliberate campaigns to oppose and eliminate all education in Christian truth and morality" (NVA, 13-14).

There is another, more profound, sense in which ours in a "post-Christian era" however. This *is* the Day of the Lord. Christ *has* come. The Kingdom *is* here, within us. Not in the fullness of its promised glory perhaps, but the promise is still there for all who accept it and live their lives accordingly. In terms of the spirituality of peace, whatever sufferings we may have to face are as nothing compared with the moral danger that lies in the temptation to repay violence with violence and, by so doing, turn away from Him and the protection He will provide. Taken in this perspective, the insane rush for security through new weapons of ever-increasing destructiveness is a betrayal of the true security which is the Christian's for the asking.

Again, in Merton's words,

> It is no exaggeration to say that our times are apocalyptic in the sense that we seem to have come to a point at which all the hidden, mysterious dynamism of the "history of salvation" revealed in the Bible has flowered into final and decisive crisis. The term "end of the world" may or may not be one that we are capable of understanding. But at any rate we seem to be assisting at the unwrapping of the mysteriously vivid symbols of the last book of the New Testament. In their nakedness, they reveal to us our own selves as the men whose lot it is to live in the time of a possibly ultimate decision. In a word, the end of the world is quite really and quite literally up to us and to our immediate descendents, if any. And this, I might venture to suggest, is more "apocalyptic" than anything our fathers discovered in the Revelation of St John (NVA, p. 13).

The three major themes, or components, of the spirituality of peace—at least as I have presented them—leave little room for Merton's (or the bishops') persistence in defending the *theory* of justifiable war. There is evidence enough in his writings that he was aware that in *practice* the traditional formulations are almost totally irrelevant to the reality of modern war and nuclear war in particular. It is tempting to speculate on where he would be today, now that bishops have re-discovered and legitimized (though not yet endorsed) the kind of pacifism he so regularly rejected. Pointless, too—for whether he accepted the label or not, his books and articles are there to provide support for those who do.

They also provide invaluable guidelines to how the spirituality of peace can be given expression in the behavior of individuals. There is an unfortunate tendency on the part of many, including pacifists, to speak in terms of a dichotomy: a choice between prayer and similar forms of spiritual activity on the one hand and involvement in direct action protests on the other.

I prefer to see the two options as the opposite ends of a single continuum with the actual positions taken located in between, each representing the "mix" of both best suited to the individual's unique "variation on the spirituality theme" or determined by the circumstances of his or her life. Thus one might expect a strictly cloistered contemplative (or the kind of isolated hermit that Merton yearned to be but never was) would have precious little opportunity or inclination to engage in outward protest, relying instead on prayer and other devotional or penitential practices to halt the drift toward the war that is forbidden. Parents, too, might find familial responsibilities too demanding to permit the "luxury" of risking arrest or prison for civil disobedience or other forms of activism. Some might even have difficulty finding the time to engage in legal demonstrations.

In neither case need protest activity be eliminated altogether. There are always letters to be written, petitions to be distributed and signed, vigils and picketting and the like to be done. Heads of households have gone further to engage in symbolic tax resistance, though few are in a position to risk their family's welfare by refusing to pay taxes altogether or renouncing taxable earnings. For their part, religious communities, in addition to participating in some kind of tax resistance, might give thought to the possibility of making themselves havens of sanctuary for "criminals of conscience"—taking as their model their counterparts in Europe which provided sanctuary for Jews and saved many from Nazi extermination camps.

Even those monasteries and convents which will concentrate on prayer and penance as their most proper expression of the spirituality of peace can reach out to the consciences of others through teaching and works of scholarship. Merton himself is the best example of what can be done in this respect. Despite the confines of the Trappist life—and even though silenced for a time by superiors who considered it "unseemly" for a monk to involve himself in public controversy—he found it possible to bring "respectability" to a position which, until then, had been dismissed by his fellow Catholics as bordering on heresy. Nor was this all. He was indirectly responsible for more direct action protest on the part of others not subject to those limitations. His 1964 retreat on "The Spiritual Roots of Protest" was especially significant. Within a short time most of his retreatants were in prison for various actions of public protest. One might go so far as to suggest that the "Great Catholic Peace Conspiracy" of the Vietnam years had its real beginning in the quiet setting of Gethsemani.

If it is difficult to conceive of prayer by itself as an effective or sufficient Christian peace witness, this is even more true of the other pole of the continuum. No matter how "extreme" or "disruptive", direct action protest can draw inspiration and support from prayer. The Berrigans and their followers offer striking evidence of how this works. In the eyes of the law, this loose and widespread network of separate but "affinity minded" groups constitute a criminal "underground". Nevertheless, all their actions—whether blocking entry to nuclear facilities, climbing fences to destroy weapons components, digging graves on the White House lawn, or pouring blood on the Pentagon—can be seen as spiritual events and experiences. They begin with sessions of common prayer and reflection in which participants make themselves open to a "call" to specific acts of civil disobedience. Once the decision is made, there is more prayer and meditation to help find the strength and confidence needed to face up to the chosen task and the penalties it could bring. Finally, after the deed is done—the blood poured, the ashes strewn, the missile cones damaged—the "criminals" join in prayer again while they await arrest.

Not all direct action is confrontational; indeed, Merton, among others, voiced concern and warned against the danger of escalation beyond peaceful protest—"in which case", as he put it, "it may also be escalating into self-contradiction". It is, again, a question of determining the right "mix" for each, which in turn depends upon that uniqueness of the individual's spirituality within the limits set by the components I have identified.

Merton was concerned that the Berrigan-type actions represented a kind of desperation that might frighten rather than edify the uncommitted public. He had a profound respect for someone like Dorothy Day who, though ever willing to refuse cooperation she felt contributed to war or the war mentality and ready to go to jail for her belief in peace, did so without seeking publicity. And he had the highest praise for a Franz Jaegerstaetter who was not "confrontational" at all but still accepted martyrdom rather than submit to the state's demand that he take part in an unjust war. It is well to note, though, he waited until he actually received induction orders to make his heroic refusal.

Anyone familiar with the lives of Dorothy Day and Franz Jaegerstaetter knows how much prayer and penance meant to them and the part these played in providing and sustaining the commitment behind Dorothy's lifelong practice of the spiritual and corporal works of mercy and Jaegerstaetter's refusal to violate his conscience. Too often, though, we write them off as exceptional cases (which, of course, they are) beyond our more normal spiritual capacities (which they are not).

It might be helpful to consider one more example to make the point. I referred earlier to John Leary, that young colleague of mine and admirer of Thomas Merton, who died of cardiac arrest at the age of 24 while jogging home from a full day of work at our Pax Christi Center to Boston's Catholic Worker soup kitchen where he lived and served the needs of

the poor and elderly. This extraordinarily gifted young man had come to Boston six years before as a Harvard freshman; when he died, his wake and funeral drew hundreds of mourners who had come to know him through the many peace and justice activities for which he had assumed personal responsibility. Though not a "leader" in the sense of public recognition, his death left our Center and a host of other organizations in a state of emotional and organizational disarray from which we have not yet recovered completely.

A review of his appointment books for the last five years of his life record the meetings he attended, demonstrations he helped arrange, talks given and workshops conducted, and innumerable other services performed and favors done. A typical week might have had as many as 15–20 such "obligations"! In addition he was arrested several times for "criminal trespass"— twice for intruding into a forbidden courtyard at a nuclear weapons laboratory to pray and distribute devotional handouts as part of the weekly vigils he helped organize—more often for "sitting in" at abortion clinics.

Remarkable as all this activism was, it was matched by the extent and intensity of his prayer life and devotional study. In taking stock of what we have lost, we find an almost perfect blending of protest and prayer. Why have I devoted so much time to him? There is the matter of emotional attachment, of course, but much more to the point, he shows what can be done. In time John Leary might have become as well-known a name as Merton, the Berrigans, and Dorothy Day and may even have surpassed them in his contributions to peace and social justice. As it was, he was just a young college student, a "worker in the ranks", who was able to make a real difference— and do so in six short years.

This should be both a comfort and a challenge to us. Not all will, or can, give equally effective expression to the spirituality of peace as a John Leary and the more widely known inspirational models I have mentioned. At best we can aspire and strive, knowing we will probably fall short. But when we do, we can renew our good intentions and strive anew. Nor will everyone agree with the pacifist interpretations I have placed on the spirituality of peace, however much those who disagree may accept and share the basic perceptions upon which it is based.

In the final analysis, the spirituality of peace is more than the perceptions from which it draws content and form, and to this extent it goes beyond the reach of sociology. The perceptions can be objectified and classified—even analyzed in terms of psychological and cultural implications; but it is the quality of commitment that counts, and this involves something extra that escapes even the most imaginative methods and techniques social science can devise. That "something extra" is the touch of grace of which Jaegerstaetter spoke, the grace which informs the intellect and strengthens the will. As Christians we believe that grace will be made available to us—if we but accept it.

A half-century ago, the eminent sociologist, Pitirim Sorokin, traced what he called "the crisis of our age" to a shift from a culture keyed to the higher realms of spirit and mind to one in which perceptions and behavior were increasingly dominated by material and sensual concerns and values. If his analysis still holds true—and I, for one, believe it does—the crisis will not be resolved unless and until the direction of this shift is reversed.

A first and necessary step would be for each of us, man or woman, to make a personal reassessment of his or her spiritual commitments and the answers we give to those three basic questions: what do I believe about God? how do I relate to God and to my fellow human beings? do I have faith enough and confidence enough to take risks He may ask of me as an individual (and of us as a people) to turn away from policies and preparations which would destroy the world and humanity to "save" them?

The answer we give will determine whether that gift of grace will be recognized as such and accepted. Merton had his answer and considered it important enough to repeat in several of his essays on the subject of peace and nuclear war.

Let it serve as the conclusion to these remarks:

> It is no longer reasonable or right to leave all decisions to a largely anonymous power elite that is driving us all, in our passivity, towards ruin. We have to make ourselves heard.
>
> Every individual Christian has a grave responsibility to protest clearly and forcibly against trends that lead inevitably to crimes which the Church deplores and condemns. Ambiguity, hesitation, and compromise are no longer permissible. We must find some new and constructive way of settling international disputes. This may be extraordinarily difficult. Obviously war cannot be abolished by mere wishing. Severe sacrifices may be demanded and the results will hardly be visible in our day. We have still time to do something about it, but the time is rapidly running out (NVA, p. 128).*

---

*This quotation and earlier ones in the present essay are from Thomas Merton's *The Nonviolent Alternative,* edited with an introduction by Gordon C. Zahn (New York: Farrar Strauss and Giroux, 1980).

Timothy Kelly

EPILOGUE:
A MEMOIR

It is a little embarrassing to be asked to present a few thoughts on Father Louis, and I feel so inadequate to the task after having been a confrere of his for ten years. In part, it is because so many capable persons have already offered insights and appraisals of Thomas Merton that my incompetence is all the more obvious, and in a certain sense may even demean the subject. But then the hesitancy may arise from the fact that there is almost something vulgar to speak of a relationship that was not in any way extraordinary, but still it was a real, private and supportive friendship. To speak of it in a public forum is more the experience of betrayal rather than the embarrassment of an inadequate presentation. However, I offer these simple memories and reflections as a sign of appreciation of my Novice Master and confrere, Thomas Merton, and hope they in no way weaken our relationship.

From my perspective, the Merton I knew was a person who

was free enough to respect each of his brother monks with a certain preference for the offbeat and rebellious in the community, and a real unwillingness to be used by others to support their personal illusions. He was a person always seeking the further shore, always longing for more life. As he described it in *The Asian Journal:* "Somehow on the edge of a great realization and knew it and . . . were trying somehow or other to go out and get lost in it" (New York: New Directions, p. 143).

The bleak December day in 1968 when Abbot Flavian Burns came to the reader's desk in the refectory at the end of the community's noon meal to announce that word had been received from the State Department a few hours previously that Father Louis had died from an accidental shock, still is vivid in the memory of many hearts. For one of the older monks, it was a very distressing moment, and he could not be certain of what he heard. The distress was caused in part by the fact that among the pieces of mail at Father Idesbald's place was a card signed simply "Brother Louis" posted a few days earlier in some exotic country, greeting Father and telling him of his future itinerary and asking his prayers. This incident has a profound meaning in a community where Father Idesbald was something of a character, produced by a system that had little respect for individuals.

Father had joined the Gethsemani community just one year after emigrating from war-torn Belgium where he spent his teenage years during World War I smuggling food for his relatives and friends. He joined a silent Gethsemani before he learned the language of the country, a monastery where communication by means of a rudimentary sign language was hardly possible for persons adept in the language and so next to impossible for someone who did not know English. Thus, Father Idesbald had a life with a lot of frustration and misunderstanding. That he could feel at ease addressing Thomas Merton and receiving a response from this brother monk half way around the world on a pilgrimage he had longed for, meeting masters of the spiritual life, and still able to remember his old brother at Gethsemani and take time to address a friendly word, says a great deal about the depth of Merton's conversion.

When I arrived at Gethsemani in 1958, unknown to me, Father Louis was Novice Master. After several days in the Guest House washing dishes and doing various chores awaiting the fateful interview with the Novice Master, the Guest Master told me to be in the room at 6:30; the Novice Master was coming. It was with relief, but with trepidation, that I awaited the time. It was a humid, late August, Kentucky evening, when in response to a knock the door was opened to a medium height, well-built monk, who laconically introduced himself as the Novice Master, and said he presumed I was the person who wanted to join. With no other name than his title, he gently asked the questions that compose such interviews. When asked if I had read anything on the life, I mentioned reading all of Merton's published works, and the works of Father Raymond (another monk of Gethsemani). In response to his question of what I thought of them, I said that "both were rather exaggerated and romantic." Merton responded: "It doesn't do to believe everything you read." Knowing my background with the Basilian Fathers, he went on to ask about the Medieval Institute in Toronto. Needless to say, I was somewhat horrified when the Father Guest Master asked me the next morning what I thought of Thomas Merton—to realize who I had been interviewed by and what I had said was the cause for great concern. A few hours later while being shown the ways of the Novitiate, we met Father Louis; I wanted to say something, but realized by the open, accepting greeting, that it was not necessary.

Our last meeting had something of the same quality. Having just returned from studies, I was doing some moral theology with the monks preparing for orders. Hurrying to Vespers from the library, I met Father Louis returning a number of books. The class was doing the morality of war, and I asked him to take part in the next day's session since he was one of the U.S.'s most vociferous critics of the war policy. He looked at me a bit quizzically—at least in retrospect it seemed so—and excused himself by saying that it is essential to have a good grasp of the Church's tradition before shooting off your mouth about present conditions. He quickly ran through the tradition and commented that: "See, even the most conservative textbook has as much to say as I have." We parted: I went to Vespers; he to the hermitage, and the next morning he left for the Far East. The questioning look came from a heart filled with boyish fear that if someone found out about the trip, and in particular our previous Abbot, Dom James Fox, he was sure the journey would be blocked. Except for the present Abbot, Father Flavian Burns, and Father Louis' personal secretary, Brother Patrick Hart, hardly anyone else was aware of the journey until he was well on his way, and certainly no one begrudged him the opportunity, knowing that he would use it well, but not without a few imprudences! That was the "Louie" we knew—imprudent, impractical, everyone's friend, and in reality, no one's possession: he was always moving on, questioning, searching, seeing and not seeing.

I was with Father Louis for almost three years in the novitiate, and returned to be his assistant the last years of his term as Novice Master. He was an excellent teacher, although always forging ahead in his thought, which was not the best for novitiate training where rudiments have to be repeated frequently. He brought an enthusiasm that was electrifying to the most arid of patristic texts, only to be utterly devastated when one went to the text on one's own and found nothing of the breadth or depth that Merton had seen. In my experience, he did not like questions in class, and handled criticisms of conferences rather poorly.

An example stands out related to modern biblical exegesis as it was referred to in the early 1960s. After Sunday Vespers we had about an hour long conference, generally on the scriptural readings of the day. At one of these he was presenting a profound and sensitive interpretation of the prophet Jonah, who was one of his favorites. Throughout the conference one of the brighter novices was continually raising his hand, but was only acknowledged at the end of the period. The novice remarked at some length on the scripture conference given to the community by Father Barnabas Ahern, C.P., in which he referred to the Jonah story as midrash. Father Louis' simple response was: "Oh!" He closed his notes, left the room never to give another extensive scriptural conference for some years.

He was very hesitant in accepting much of the scriptural work available in English in the early 1960s. His criticism of it as foundational for the spiritual life was harsh. His heart was patristic, his emotions responded to the beauty and order of the high middle ages—and modern jazz! The only display of emotion was at a Sunday conference a few days after Christmas as he read from the last lines of T. S. Eliot's *Murder in the Cathedral,* where Thomas says the famous lines: "The last temptation is the greatest treason: to do the right thing for the wrong reason." The conference had to be stopped because of tears, and he went on to a different subject.

He loved the Latin Liturgy, and walked out of the Palm Sunday Liturgy when the Passion was read in English for the first time. (Since then we have very sensitive renditions of the English in chant). He celebrated the Eucharist in Latin whenever possible. Among the possessions returned with his body from Bangkok were a number of relics: Bede the Venerable, Saint Bruno, Thomas of Canterbury, Charbel, Saint Therese and others. He was a pious person in the best sense of the word with a deep personal relation to the Vulgate Scriptures, even though they were considered technically inferior to more recent texts. He prayed a few psalms each day as private devotion.

Father Louis' disdain for modern farm equipment was well-known to the community. It was the source of well-accepted teasing, when the whole convoy of the monastery's heavy equipment had to be engaged to move a number of large boulders several miles to be properly arranged in the Zen garden for the Novice Master. On doctor appointment days, the last directive given for the day's work was generally to get the caterpillar to the hermitage to clean up the brush or the lawn mowers to cut the grass. As in so many aspects of his life, contradictions abounded in the practical area also, sometimes to our exasperation, but always with a guileless surprise on his part as to why we should be so concerned.

One bright, sunny, March afternoon Father Louis and I were using axes and brush-hooks to clean an area of woods when a gigantic B-52 flew very low directly over us visibly quivering in the strong March wind. The strategic air command flew regularly in the area near Fort Knox in the mid-sixties. After the deafening noise passed, I commented to Father that, prescinding from the use of this machine, it was fantastic to realize that such a thing could be made by human beings, and how a machine such as this must affect cultures that have not gone through the long development to arrive at this point. He went off on a long tirade about the cultural bankruptcy such a monstrosity signifies, and on and on. Interesting to contrast with this with the description of the planes lining up for take-off in the opening pages of *The Asian Journal:* "The slow ballet of tailfins in the sun . . . A quadrille of planes jockeying for place . . . The moment of takeoff was ecstatic . . . The window wept jagged shining courses of tears. Joy". This does not seem to refer to "cultural bankruptcy" and has an entirely different feel toward airplanes than our conversation five years earlier in the woods of Kentucky leaning on our axes!

The contradictions, ambiguities, inconsistencies, misplaced enthusiasms, or just too much enthusiasm, were Father Louis. In part, they hid the depths of the person, and in another sense showed the reality of the very human person. But over the long term, it was difficult to respond to all his enthusiasms, for us lesser souls cannot hold so much divergent material in a living form. Father Louis sometimes had to be not considered just in order that we might have space to live and also that he might have space. But he felt this. Yet, from another perspective, that was the way he would have wanted it. He always respected individual persons, and in the novitiate formation he encouraged us in self-knowledge and discernment of our personal way of living the Gospel. He emphasized in his own non-directive way the importance of knowing our true selves in order to respond to our particular grace, that salvation and sanctification were not to be found in some perfect form, but rather in our total response to the gifts given to us personally.

His instructions to the novices were based on the monastic tradition, much of which he was making available in English for the first time. His approach to the ascetic discipline of Trappist tradition created a new climate within the community with some ramifications throughout the Order. Rather than seeing the ascetic life as penance for sins, our personal sins or those of the world, he taught an asceticism that in the best Benedictine tradition calls the monk to an expansion of heart that allows his life to be no more his own, but Christ living in him. His ascetic principles demanded that we see the beauty of nature, to enjoy the simple food that is a part of daily living, and always to be completely present at whatever one was doing. From his own example, he taught us to laugh at ourselves, and the absurd things we often do. This he always did with an element of freedom.

His conferences often had insightful comments on present political situations, but presented as something to be aware of to deepen our spiritual response and to grow in compassion for our suffering brothers and sisters. His politics were obviously liberal, and here, too, enthusiasms sometimes placed him in awkward situations.

He was constantly writing, thinking with his pen, but it was not something that he encouraged the novices to do, nor did he ever portray himself as a tortured self-reflective person in his community living. The amount of his published works, the extent of his correspondence, comes almost as a surprise to many of us since it was not all that obvious that he was writing.

He always encouraged respect and fidelity to superiors.

223

Though I was his assistant at a time when he was in something of a crisis with authorities in the Order, he never complained to me, nor showed any lack of responsible obedience. When I complained to him, he was quick to call me to a respectful obedience. He could be abrupt in his dealings with others, sometimes showing impatience but never anger. When a conversation was completed, one was quickly dismissed. Small talk was not a part of his community life.

While a student in Rome, news from Gethsemani gave me many concerns about the changes taking place. I addressed my observations to Father Louis in his hermitage. He responded, clarifying some factual information, acknowledging the reality of my concerns, and excusing his own lack of speaking up as being a consequence of living very much on the fringe of the community, the way he wanted it. He was quick to point out that I was doing the same thing that I complained about concerning the community leadership. I presented my position, my truth, in the same absolute terms, with the same veiled threats that others did. Then he spoke of an essential element of religious life, something that took him twenty-five years to learn, and that it is very difficult to speak of—and that is compromise. The word itself in English bears a significance that seems far from a source of spiritual living, but yet he felt it was the most important element to learn in order to continue to grow. Then he commented, but did not develop it, that the great task of the Church was to develop a true theology of love.

The burial of Father Louis on a rainy evening on the 17th of December, 1968, had elements of Resurrection faith that were true to his character. But for me, there was something of an experience of incompletion, still on the edge of a great realization. This convinces me of the accidental character of his death, probably by electric shock from a faulty fan. The arrival of the body had many of the inconsistencies that were so much a part of our brother. The outspoken pacifist was flown to the U.S. in a military transport, in a military coffin, with a military blanket for a shroud, surrounded by dead Vietnam heroes. The difficulties in getting the corpse through immigration would have been a great joke for our brother, Louis, arriving late for his own Funeral!

The question is often presented to Father Louis' community, whether he is a saint. What are the criterions of sanctity? If it is the simple Gospel dictum about giving a cup of water to the needy, there is no doubt. The example of Father Idesbald's card, and so many other small kindnesses to men who knew little of such thoughtfulness are examples of Gospel living.

If we use some complex series of tests about living in ways and conditions foreign to one's natural orientation as a sign of sanctity, again there is little doubt that Father Louis was heroic in this area. Gethsemani in the 1940s was pretty grim, and certainly very, very few of the monks came from the cultural or educational background that had been Thomas Merton's daily life.

If we use as the model for sanctity a person who went against or beyond his natural inclinations, again there are many obvious signs of sanctity. To say that he practised simple virtue to a heroic degree is no exaggeration. To say that he was tempted and may have failed only says that he was human. To realize that he was always completely honest about any failure, is perhaps the clearest sign of sanctity, and the element in our brother, Father Louis' life, from which all of us can best learn.

Still, in the depths of my heart there is a feeling that there was something more to be done. But perhaps that was done in the "going out and getting lost in the great realization".

NOTES

INTRODUCTION

1. Personal recollections of a monk of Gethsemani.
2. Thomas Merton, *The Monastic Journey,* edited by Brother Patrick Hart (Mission, Kan.: Sheed, Andrews, and McMeel, 1977), p. 165.
3. *Ibid.*
4. *Ibid.,* p. 167.
5. *Ibid.*
6. Merton, "An Exchange of Letters on Monastic Questions", (Gethsemani, Ky.: Abbey of Gethsemani, 1963), p. 24.
7. *Ibid.*
8. *Ibid.,* p. 25.
9. *Ibid.*
10. Merton, *Contemplation in a World of Action* (N.Y.: Doubleday, 1971), p. 141.
11. *Ibid.,* pp. 141-42.
12. Merton, *The Collected Poems of Thomas Merton* (N.Y.: New Directions, 1978).
13. Merton, *Seeds of Destruction,* (N.Y.: Farrar, Straus and Giroux, 1964), p. 319.
14. Merton, *Contemplation in a World of Action,* p. 182.
15. *Ibid.,* p. 183.
16. Merton, *The Monastic Journey,* p. 131. Cf. also Brother Patrick Hart (ed.), *Thomas Merton/Monk* (Kalamazoo: Cistercian Publications, 1983), pp. 173-93.
17. Merton, *The Monastic Journey,* p. 131.
18. Merton, *Contemplation in a World of Action,* p. 223.
19. *Ibid.,* p. 225.
20. *Ibid.,* p. 338.
21. *Ibid.*
22. *Ibid.,* p. 374.
23. *Ibid.,* pp. 374-75.
24. Merton, Letter to the Editor, *National Catholic Reporter,* January 11, 1968, "Regaining the Old Monastic Charism," p. 11.
25. *Ibid.*
26. *Ibid.*
27. Merton, "The Council and Monasticism", in *The Impact of Vatican II,* edited by Jude P. Dougherty (N.Y.: Herder, 1966), p. 51.
28. *Ibid.,* pp. 51-52.

29. *Ibid.,* p. 49.
30. Merton, "A Conference on Prayer", in *Sisters Today* XLI (1970), pp. 449-56.
31. Merton, *Contemplation in a World of Action,* p. 337.
32. Merton, "The Council and Monasticism", p. 54.
33. Merton, *Contemplation in a World of Action,* p. 8.
34. *Ibid.,* pp. 8-9.
35. *Ibid.,* p. 9.
36. *Ibid.,* p. xx; cf. *Thomas Merton/Monk,* pp. 93-124.
37. Merton, *The Asian Journal of Thomas Merton,* edited by Brother Patrick Hart, Naomi Burton, and James Laughlin (N.Y.: New Directions, 1973), p. 329.
38. *Ibid.*
39. *Ibid.,* p. 306.
40. *Ibid.*

WITHIN A TRADITION OF PRAYER

1. Thomas Merton, *The Climate of Monastic Prayer,* Spencer, Mass., Cistercian Publications (Cistercian Studies Series, Number 1), 1969; p. 51.
2. John J. Higgins, *Merton's Theology of Prayer,* Spencer, Mass., Cistercian Publications (Cistercian Studies Series Number 18), 1971; p. 115.
3. Cf. RB 52:4; something of this matter is sketched out in a forthcoming article on *Intentio cordis.*
4. Cf. Donald Heinz, "The Consuming Self", *America* 4 June 1977; pp. 498-500.
5. Thomas Merton, Foreword to William Johnston's *The Mysticism of the Cloud of Unknowing,* New York, Desclée Company, 1967; p. xiii.
6. *The Climate,* p. 93.
7. *Ibid.,* pp. 145-146.
8. *Ibid.,* p. 48.
9. Thomas Merton, *The New Man,* London, Burns and Oates, 1962; p. 30.
10. Thomas Merton, *Inner Experience,* p. 6; quoted in Raymond Bailey, *Thomas Merton on Mysticism,* Garden City, Doubleday, 1975; p. 139. [This MS. has been published in *Cistercian Studies* serially during 1983 and 1984 in eight installments.]
11. *The Climate,* p. 40.
12. "But it was through his study of the early Cistercians that Merton was to be led to further contact with some of the great Greek theologians and mystics". J.E. Bamberger, "Thomas Merton and the

Christian East", in M. Basil Pennington (ed.), *One Yet Two: Monastic Tradition East and West,* Kalamazoo, Mich., Cistercian Publications (Cistercian Studies Series, Number 29), 1976, 440-451; p. 443.

13. Thomas Merton, "Openness and Cloister" in *Contemplation in a World of Action,* London, George Allen and Unwin Ltd, 1971, 129-142. The article had already appeared in *Cistercian Studies* 2 (1967) 312-323.

THE FAR EAST

1. For detailed information, see Marquita Breit, *Thomas Merton: A Bibliography* (New Jersey: The Scarecrow Press, 1974). [An updated and enlarged edition of this Merton Bibliography is being published by Garland Press, New York, in 1986.]

2. D. T. Suzuki, *The Field of Zen,* Ed. by Christmas Humphreys, (New York, Harper and Row, 1970), p. xi.

3. The "Man of No Title" is called also the "Zen Man", or the "Inner Man" by Master Rinzai. Cf. Erich Fromm and D. T. Suzuki, *Zen Buddhism and Psychoanalysis* (New York: Harper and Row, 1970), pp. 32-43.

4. T. Merton, *Zen and the Birds of Appetite* (New York: New Directions, 1968), pp. 60-61.

5. *Ibid.,* p. 99.

6. Thomas Merton, *Wisdom of the Desert* (New York: New Directions, 1960), p. 1.

7. *Ibid.,* pp. 5, 7.

8. D. T. Suzuki, *Essays in Zen Buddhism,* Third Series (N.Y.: Samuel Weiser, 1971), p. 248.

9. Joseph Campbell, *The Masks of God: Primitive Mythology* (New York: Penguin Books, 1977), p. 53.

10. Ernest Wood, *Zen Dictionary* (Rutland: C. Tuttle, 1972), p. 139.

11. D. T. Suzuki, *Essays in Zen Buddhism,* Third Series, p. 89.

12. D. T. Suzuki, *Mysticism, Christian and Buddhist* (New York: Harper and Row, 1971), pp. 145, 150.

13. Zenkei Shibayama, *Zen Comment on the Mumonkan,* transl. by Sumiko Kudo (New York: A Mentor Book, 1974), p. 113.

14. Joshu Sasaki Roshi, *Conferences Given at Saint Joseph's Abbey,* Spencer, Mass., Conference no. 1.

15. T. Merton, *Zen and the Birds of Appetite,* p. 105.

16. *Ibid.,* p. 100.

17. T. Merton, *Zen and the Birds of Appetite,* p. 115.

18. D. T. Suzuki, *Essays in Zen Buddhism,* First Series (London: Rider and Company, 1970), p. 273-274.

19. T. Merton, *Zen and the Birds of Appetite,* p. 110.

20. *Ibid.,* p. 110.

21. *Ibid.,* p. 110.

22. Suzuki also wrote: "It is out of this zero that all good is performed and all evil is avoided. The zero I speak of is not a mathematical symbol. It is the infinite a storehouse or womb (Garbba) of all possible good values." T. Merton, *Zen and the Birds of Appetite,* p. 107.

23. D. T. Suzuki, *Essays in Zen Buddhism.* Third Series, p. 252.

24. Casimir Kucharek, *The Sacramental Mysteries* (New Jersey: Alleluia Press, 1976), p. 360.

25. T. Merton, *Zen and the Birds of Appetite,* p. 133.

26. T. Merton, *Zen and the Birds of Appetite,* p. 139.

27. *Ibid.,* p. 138.

28. T. Merton, *Zen and the Birds of Appetite,* p. 62.

29. See: Joshu Sasaki Roshi, *Buddha, the Center of Gravity of the Universe* (New Mexico: Lama Foundation, 1974), pp. 28, 48.

30. See Zenkei Shibayama, *Zen Comment on the Mumonkan,* p. 229 ff.

31. Erich Fromm and D. T. Suzuki, *Zen Buddhism and Psychoanalysis,* p. 75.

32. *The Way of Lao-Tzu,* transl. by Wing Tsi Chan (Indianapolis: Bobbs Merrill, 1963), pp. 97, 124, 162.

33. *John* 14:6.

34. See D. T. Suzuki, *Essays in Zen Buddhism,* Third Series, p. 89.

35. See Thomas Merton, *The Asian Journal.* Ed. by Naomi Burton, Brother Patrick Hart, O.C.S.O., and others (New York: New Directions, 1973), pp. 58-59, 233-234.

36. See Thomas Merton, *Hagia Sophia* (Kentucky: Stamperia del Sanctuccio, 1962, 8 p.) a short but excellent prose poem in which T. Merton personified "Wisdom", and compare Merton's notion of Wisdom as Sister with D. T. Suzuki's Prajna as Mother, in *Essays in Zen Buddhism,* Third Series, pp. 246-251.

PILGRIM: FREEDOM BOUND
All notes within the text.

HIGH CULTURE AND SPIRITUALITY

1. Lawrence S. Cunningham. "The Life of Merton as Paradigm", in *The Message of Thomas Merton,* ed. Patrick Hart, (Kalamazoo: Cistercian Publications, 1981), pp. 154-65.

2. "The Aesthetics of Silence", in *The Susan Sontag Reader* (New York: Farrar, Straus, and Giroux, 1982), p. 181.

3. Sontag, p. 189.

4. I am, for purposes of this paper, using the tradition of modernism as the equivalent of "high culture" but not in any strict sociological sense.

5. "Five Unpublished Letters from Ad Reinhardt to Thomas Merton and Two in Return", *Art Forum* (December, 1978), p. 24.

6. *The Asian Journal of Thomas Merton*, eds. Naomi Burton, Patrick Hart, and James Laughlin (New York: New Directions, 1973), p. 233.

7. *Asian Journal*, pp. 235-36.

8. "Roland Barthes—Writing as Temperature", in *The Literary Essays of Thomas Merton*, ed. Patrick Hart. (New York: New Directions, 1981), p. 144.

9. *Ibid.,* p. 146.

10. Sister Thérèse Lentfoehr, *Words and Silence: On The Poetry of Thomas Merton* (New York: New Directions, 1981), p. 103.

11. Cf. The "Author's Note" in *Collected Poems* (New York: New Directions, 1977), p. 455.

12. In his "Poetry and Contemplation: A Reappraisal", *Literary Essays,* pp. 338-354. First published in 1958 he eschews views he held (and wrote about) ten years previously.

13. Sontag, p. 203.

A MONASTIC EXCHANGE OF LETTERS: LECLERCQ AND MERTON
References to the Leclercq and Merton letters within the text.

POETRY AS EXEMPLIFICATION OF THE MONASTIC JOURNEY

1. While there have been considerable studies of Merton's poetry this particular theme has thus far only been approached obliquely. See: for example, the recent books of George Woodcock, *Thomas Merton, Monk and Poet. A critical study.* (New York: Farrar, Straus, and Giroux, 1978); Sister Thérèse Lentfoehr, *Words and Silence, On the Poetry of Thomas Merton* (New York: New Directions, 1979); and Ross Labrie, *The Art of Thomas Merton* (Fort Worth: Texas Christian University, 1979), all of which are valuable, but which focus on other aspects of Merton's writing.

2. For a detailed consideration of Merton's life and work as continuing conversion see the recent book by Sister Elena Malits, *The Solitary Explorer, Thomas Merton's Transforming Journey* (New York: Harper and Row, 1980).

3. *The Collected Poems of Thomas Merton* (New York: New Directions, 1977), p. 193. Subsequent references are noted parenthetically.

4.   *Thoughts in Solitude,* (New York: Farrar, Straus and Giroux, 1978), p. 87.

5.   See, for example, pp. 20, 111, pp. 349-362 in *The Sign of Jonas* (New York: Harcourt, Brace and Co., 1953).

6.   *Ibid.,* p. 72.

7.   See, *The Way of Chuang Tzu* (New York: New Directions 1965) which includes a long interpretive wtudy by Merton, pp. 13-32.

8.   First published in 1953; available in paperback from The Liturgical Press, Collegeville, Minnesota. See also Merton's pamphlet *Praying the Psalms* (Collegeville: The Liturgical Press, 1965).

THE SOLITARY LIFE

1.   James Forest, *Thomas Merton: A Pictorial Biography* (New York: Paulist Press, 1980), p. 85.

2.   Thomas Merton, "Night-Flowering Cactus", *The Collected Poems of Thomas Merton* (New York: New Directions, 1977), p. 352.

3.   Thomas Merton, *Contemplation in a World of Action* (Garden City, New York: Doubleday Image Books, 1973), p. 245.

4.   Forest, *Thomas Merton: A Pictorial Biography,* p. 85.

5.   Patrick Hart, editor, *Thomas Merton/Monk—A Monastic Tribute* (Garden City, New York: Doubleday Image Books, 1976), pp. 41-42. [This volume was reissued in an enlarged edition by Cistercian Publications in 1983.]

6.   Merton, *The Seven Storey Mountain,* pp. 422-423.

7.   Thomas Merton, *The Sign of Jonas* (Garden City, New York: Doubleday Image Books, 1956), p. 20.

8.   *Ibid.,* p. 227.

9.   Monica Furlong, *Merton: A Biography* (San Francisco: Harper and Row, 1980), p. 205.

10.   Thomas Merton to Dom Jean Leclercq, 10 August 1955, The Thomas Merton Studies Center, Louisville, Kentucky.

11.   Hart, *Thomas Merton/Monk,* p. 68.

12.   *Ibid.,* p. 153.

13.   Thomas Merton, *Thoughts in Solitude* (Garden City, New York: Doubleday Image Books, 1968), p. 102.

14.   Thomas Merton, *Disputed Questions* (New York: Farrar, Straus and Giroux, 1977), p. 152.

15.   *Ibid.,* p. 156.

16.   *The Wisdom of the Desert,* with a foreword, and trans. by, Thomas Merton (New York: New Directions, 1970), pp. 3-4.

17.   *Ibid.,* p. 23.

18.   Timothy Fry, editor, *The Rule of St. Benedict* (Collegeville,

Minnesota: The Liturgical Press, 1981), p. 169.

19. Merton, *Disputed Questions,* p. 161.

20. Thomas Merton, *The Monastic Journey,* edited by Patrick Hart (Garden City, New York: Doubleday Image Books, 1977), p. 197.

21. Merton, "Song: If You Seek . . . " *The Collected Poems,* p. 340.

22. Patrick Hart, editor, *The Message of Thomas Merton* (Kalamazoo, Michigan: Cistercian Publications, 1981), p. 118.

23. Thomas Merton, *New Seeds of Contemplation* (New York: New York: New Directions, 1961), p. 81.

24. Merton, *Contemplation in a World of Action,* p. 270.

25. Merton, *Disputed Questions,* p. 187.

26. *Ibid.,* p. 189.

27. Merton, *Love and Living,* p. 20.

28. Merton, *New Seeds of Contemplation,* p. 65.

29. Thomas Merton, *The Silent Life* (New York: Farrar, Straus and Giroux, 1976), p. 18.

30. *Ibid.,* p. 18.

31. A. Hallier, *Introduction to the Monastic Theology of Aelred of Rievaulx* by Thomas Merton (Kalamazoo, Michigan: Cistercian Publications, 1969), p. x.

32. Thomas Merton, *The New Man* (New York: Farrar, Straus and Giroux, 1980), p. 149.

33. Merton, *Disputed Questions,* p. 192.

34. Merton, *Contemplation in a World of Action,* p. 258.

35. James Finley, *Merton's Palace of Nowhere* (Notre Dame, Indiana: Ave Maria Press, 1978), p. 134.

36. Thomas Merton, "Day of a Stranger", *The Hudson Review* 20 (Summer 1967), p. 215.

37. *Ibid.,* p. 215.

38. Thomas Merton, "The Solitary Life", *Cistercian Studies* 4 (1969): 214.

39. Merton, *Thoughts in Solitude,* p. 86.

40. Merton, *The Monastic Journey,* p. 201.

41. *Ibid.,* p. 152.

42. Merton, *Disputed Questions,* p. 186.

43. John Howard Griffin, *The Hermitage Journals* (Kansas City: Andrews and McMeel), p. 21.

44. Merton, "The Solitary Life", p. 217.

A COINCIDENCE OF OPPOSITES
All notes within the text.

SOURCES AND SIGNS OF SPIRITUAL GROWTH

1. James Olney, *Metaphors of Self: The Meaning of Autobiography* (Princeton, N.J.: Princeton University Press, 1972), pp. 31-32.
2. Roy Pascal, *Design and Truth in Autobiography* (Cambridge, Mass.: Harvard University Press, 1969), p. 182.
3. *The Asian Journal of Thomas Merton* (New York: New Directions Books, 1973), p. 296.
4. Merton, *Faith and Violence* (Notre Dame, Ind.: University of Notre Dame Press, 1963), p. 213.
5. Merton, "Day of a Stranger", in *A Thomas Merton Reader* (revised edition), ed. Thomas P. McDonnell (New York: Image Books, 1974), p. 431.
6. Merton, *Faith and Violence*, p. 219 and *The Asian Journal*, p. 312.
7. Merton, *The Sign of Jonas* (New York: Image Books, 1956), pp. 20-21.
8. Merton, *The Seven Storey Mountain* (New York: Signet Books, 1948), p. 400.
9. Merton, *The Sign of Jonas*, pp. 228-229.
10. Merton, *Conjectures of a Guilty Bystander* (New York: Image Books, 1968), p. 5.
11. *Ibid.*, p. 67.
12. *Ibid.*, p. 6.
13. *Ibid.*, p. 7.
14. *Ibid.*, pp. 156-157.
15. *Ibid.*, p. 7.

ECCLESIOLOGICAL DEVELOPMENT

1. Merton, *The Seven Storey Mountain* (New York: Doubleday, 1970), p. 19.
2. *Ibid.*, p. 23.
3. *Ibid.*, pp. 70-1.
4. *Ibid.*, pp. 84-5.
5. *Ibid.*, pp. 85-6.
6. *Ibid.*, pp. 253-4.
7. *Ibid.*, p. 146.
8. *Ibid.*, pp. 229-30.
9. *Ibid.*, p. 112.
10. *Ibid.*, p. 208.
11. Merton, *Conjectures of a Guilty Bystander* (New York: Doubleday, 1968), p. 89.

234

12. Merton, "What Is the Monastic Life?" in *The Monastic Journey*, edited by Brother Patrick Hart (New York: Doubleday, 1978), p. 25.

13. "Monastic Peace", *Ibid.,* p. 84. Cf. also "Basic Principles of Monastic Theology", *Ibid.,* pp. 35-6 (Both essays reprinted in *The Monastic Journey*).

14. Merton, *The Seven Storey Mountain,* p. 86.

15. "Monastic Peace", in *The Monastic Journey,* p. 85. In "What Is the Monastic Life?", he writes: "Jesus clearly promised that He would be truly and objectively present in His Church, as its ruler, sanctifier and teacher but particularly in this most concrete and most spiritual of all actions: His own High-priestly sacrifice of the Mass. Christ Jesus is then our priest and our victim, and it is He who mystically offers Mass among us, just as truly present in the midst of the faithful today as He was in the midst of His disciples at the Last Supper". *Ibid.,* pp. 25-6.

16. Merton, *The Seven Storey Mountain,* p. 52.

17. *Ibid.,* p. 70-1.

18. *Ibid.,* p. 411.

19. *Ibid.,* p. 242. Cf. also *The Literary Essays of Thomas Merton,* edited with an introduction by Brother Patrick Hart (New York: New Directions, 1981), Appendix II.

20. *Ibid.,* p. 218.

21. "Basic Principles of Monastic Spirituality" in *The Monastic Journey,* p. 33. Cf. also Merton, *The Sign of Jonas* (New York: Doubleday, 1956), p. 86.

22. *Ibid.,* p. 51.

23. *Ibid.,* p. 48.

24. *Ibid.*

25. Merton, *The Sign of Jonas,* p. 140.

26. *Ibid.,* p. 198.

27. *Ibid.,* p. 221.

28. Merton also acknowledged his affinity for the works of Dom Odo Casel and Louis Bouyer on the priesthood. Cf. *Ibid.,* p. 189.

29. Even Merton's exposure to Eastern Christianity's theology and liturgy contained elements of the Pauline idea of the Body of Christ and, as he remarked, the Eastern rite "gives you a greater sense of the reality of the Mystical Body. There is a much more vital participation between celebrants and people . . . . Our liturgy is too private". *Ibid.,* pp. 134-5.

30. Merton, *The Seven Storey Mountain,* pp. 209-10.

31. *Ibid.,* pp. 254-5.

32. *Ibid.,* pp. 208-9.

33. Merton, *Conjectures of a Guilty Bystander,* p. 318.

34. *Ibid.,* p. 49.

35. *Ibid.,* p. 261. Speaking of Pope John XXIII, Merton wrote, in 1963, on the eve of the Pope's death that "for many people he has restored hope in the Church as a living reality, as the true Body of Christ. He has made the reality of the Spirit in the world once more simply and profoundly credible even to people who are not easily disposed to believe in anything". *Ibid.,* pp. 301-2.

36. "One of the things most wrong about the exaggerated legalism and institutionalism in the Catholic Church today is this attempt to dominate Christians by fear—the implication that if they do not submit to complete overcontrol they will cease to exist as true human beings and as members of Christ. This is so manifestly false that some Catholics are literally driven away from the visible Church in which they cannot, in conscience, meet some exorbitant demand stupidly forced on them by incompetent officials. The man who can live happily without snuggling up at every moment to some person, institution, or vice is there as a promise of freedom for the rest of men". Merton, "Christian Solitude", in *Contemplation in a World of Action* (New York: Doubleday, 1973), pp. 259-60.

37. Merton, *Conjectures of a Guilty Bystander,* pp. 156-7.

38. Merton, "Openness and Cloister", in *Contemplation in a World of Action,* p. 155.

39. Cf. "Is the World a Problem?" in *Ibid.,* pp. 161-5.

40. *Ibid.,* p. 163.

41. Merton, *Conjectures of a Guilty Bystander,* p. 46.

42. *Ibid.,* p. 318.

43. *Ibid.,* pp. 318-19.

44. Cf. note 33 above.

45. *Ibid.,* p. 116.

46. "Monastic Peace", in *The Monastic Journey,* pp. 109-10.

47. "In the whole question of the (Catholic) Church and the world, we come again and again to the various ways in which adaptation to 'the world' can in fact be an expression of shame and fear—guilt at having failed to 'hold' the modern world and to charm it with spectacles, pageantry, lively new debates, and other contrivances. To be dominated by the fear of losing our 'hold' on men, especially on youth, is implicitly to confront the world in abject shame at the name and power of Christ. We do not preach Christ, we preach our own modernity, our own cleverness, our liveliness, our fashionableness, and our charm . . . " . Merton, *Conjectures of a Guilty Bystander,* p. 125. Cf. also *Ibid.,* p. 53; p. 325.

48. *Ibid.,* p. 46.

49. *Ibid.,* p. 325.

50. *Ibid.,* pp. 325-6.

51. Merton, *Mystics and Zen Masters* (New York: Dell Publishing Co., Inc., 1967), p. 272.

52. Merton, *The Seven Storey Mountain,* pp. 413-14.

53. Leslie Dewart, "A Post-Christian Age?" (Dialogue with Merton), *Continuum* I (Winter 1964), p. 564.

54. Merton, *Faith and Violence* (Indiana: University of Notre Dame Press, 1968), p. 161.

55. *Ibid.,* p. 64. Cf. also pp. 148-9.

56. "If the Church allowed the word of God to be sharper than a two-edged sword . . . it might help white people to see that the very hysteria of their attack on the Negro is the evidence of an uneasy conscience".—Reinhold Niebuhr. Merton, *Conjectures of a Guilty Bystander,* p. 243.

57. Merton, *Faith and Violence,* p. 66.

58. Merton, *Mystics and Zen Masters,* p. 85.

59. Merton, *The Seven Storey Mountain,* p. 76.

60. *Ibid.,* p. 107.

61. Merton, *Contemplation in a World of Action,* p. 251.

THE SPIRITUALITY OF PEACE
All notes within the text.

EPILOGUE: A MEMOIR
All notes within the text.

NOTES ON CONTRIBUTORS

MICHAEL CASEY, OCSO, a monk of Tarrawarra Abbey in Australia, is an Associate Editor of *Cistercian Studies*. He completed his doctoral work at the Melbourne College of Divine with a study of desire for God in St Bernard of Clairvaux. He has lectured extensively to Benedictine and Cistercian communities around the world, and has been a member of the commission charged with writing new Constitutions of the Cistercians of the Strict Observance.

JOSEPH CHU-CONG, OCSO, a native of Vietnam, has served the community of St Joseph's Abbey, Spencer, Massachusetts, for many years as novice master. At present, he is living with the Cistercian monastery of Our Lady of the Philippines in Iloilo, Guimaras Island. His article on Thomas Merton and the Far East first appeared in the memorial issue of *Cistercian Studies* which marked the tenth anniversary of Merton's death.

HILARY COSTELLO, OCSO, a monk of Mount Saint Bernard Abbey in England, entered the monastery in 1947 at the age of twenty-one. He was ordained to the priesthood in August, 1955, and worked for several years editing the Latin texts of the Cistercian Fathers, chiefly Guerric of Igny and John of Ford (English versions in the Cistercian Fathers Series). He has written many articles on these subjects. At present he is editor of *Hallel*.

LAWRENCE S. CUNNINGHAM is Professor of Religion at Florida State University and the author of several books, including *The Meaning of Saints, St Francis of Assisi,* and a two-volume textbook on *Culture and Values.* His special interest, manifested in his most recent book *The Catholic Heritage* (Crossroad, 1984) is the relationship of Western culture and Catholic tradition.

PATRICK HART, OCSO, a monk of Gethsemani Abbey since 1951, has edited a number of books by and about Thomas Merton in the years since Merton's death. These include *Thomas Merton, Monk: A Monastic Tribute* and *The Message of Thomas Merton* (Cistercian Publications, 1981 and 1983). He is editor of *Cistercian Studies* and of the present volume.

VICTOR A. KRAMER is Professor of English at Georgia State University, Atlanta, where he teaches American literature and literary criticism. His publications include books on James Agee, Frederick Law Olmsted, and the writers Andrew Lytle, Walker Percy, and Peter Taylor. His many articles on Thomas Merton have appeared in *The Journal of the American Academy of Religion, Studia Mystica, Review, Christianity and Literature, American Benedictine Review, Commonweal, Resources for American Literary Study,* and *Cross Currents.* His book on the literary career of Merton appeared in the Twayne United States Authors Series in 1984. Currently he is working on an oral history of Thomas Merton and contemporary monasticism.

DOROTHY LEBEAU, a registered nurse by profession, is continuing her studies in theology, and plans to do her doctoral work on some aspect of Thomas Merton's Spirituality. The present article is based on her Master of Arts in Spirituality thesis at St Louis University, St Louis, Missouri.

JEAN LECLERCQ, OSB, is a monk of Clervaux Abbey, Luxembourg, a monastic scholar and historian, and the critical editor of the works of St Bernard of Clairvaux. In addition to his numerous books and articles in French and Italian, he is well known among English readers for *The Love of Learning and the Desire for God, Alone with God, The Way of Perfection, Aspects of Monasticism, Contemplative Life, Monks and Love in the Twelfth Century,* and *Monks on Marriage.*

ELENA MALITS, CSC, a sister of Holy Cross, has taught Merton seminars for many years at St Mary's College, Notre Dame. Her doctoral thesis at Fordham University formed the basis of her book *The Solitary Explorer: Thomas Merton's Transforming Journey* (Harper and Row, 1980).

MARY L. SCHNEIDER, OSF, a member of the Sisters of St Francis of Assisi of Milwaukee, Wisconsin, received her PhD in Religious Studies from Marquette University and is Associate Professor of Religious Studies at Michigan State University. She has chaired the Consultation on Thomas Merton unit of the American Academy of Religion and published extensively in the area of American civil religion, including "A Catholic Perspective on American Civil Religion" in T. McFadden, ed., *America in Theological Perspective* (1976), and "American Civil Religion and the National Catholic Rural Life Conference" in D. Alvarez, ed., *An American Church* (1979).

GORDON C. ZAHN is Professor Emeritus of the University of Massachusetts (Boston) and Director of the Pax Cristi USA Center on Conscience and War. A Catholic pacifist during World War II, he edited

Thomas Merton's *The Nonviolent Alternative,* and has written *German Catholics and Hitler's War* and *In Solitary Witness: The Life and Death of Franz Jaegerstaetter.* He served as a consultant for the American Bishops' pastoral letter on peace.

TIMOTHY KELLY, OCSO, a native of Windsor, Ontario, has been a monk of Gethsemani Abbey since 1958, and was thus a novice under Thomas Merton, later serving as Undermaster of Novices. After studies in canon law and moral theology in Rome, he returned to Gethsemani as Novice Master until he was elected Abbot in 1973.

CISTERCIAN PUBLICATIONS INC.
Kalamazoo, Michigan

TITLES LISTING

THE CISTERCIAN FATHERS SERIES

THE WORKS OF
BERNARD OF CLAIRVAUX

THE WORKS OF WILLIAM OF
SAINT THIERRY

THE WORKS OF
AELRED OF RIEVAULX

THE WORKS OF GILBERT OF
HOYLAND

THE WORKS OF JOHN OF FORD

Texts and Studies
in the
Monastic Tradition

Temporarily out of print   †*Forthcoming*

Temporarily out of print   † *Forthcoming*